Sloth Coloring Book for Adults

By Peaceful Mind Adult Coloring Books

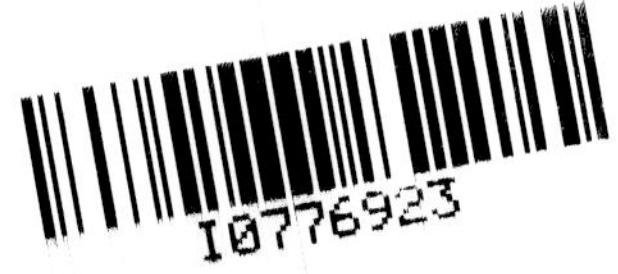

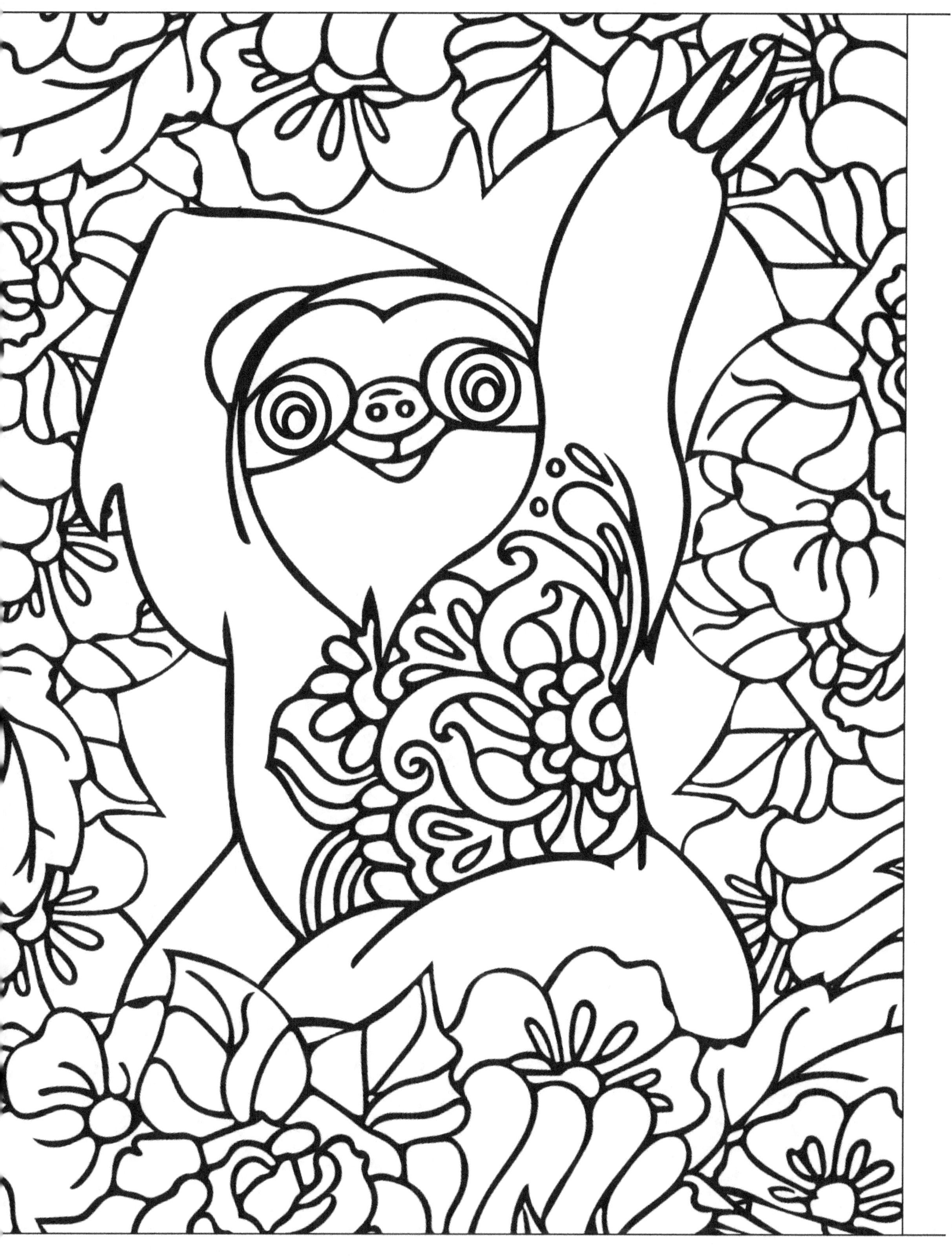

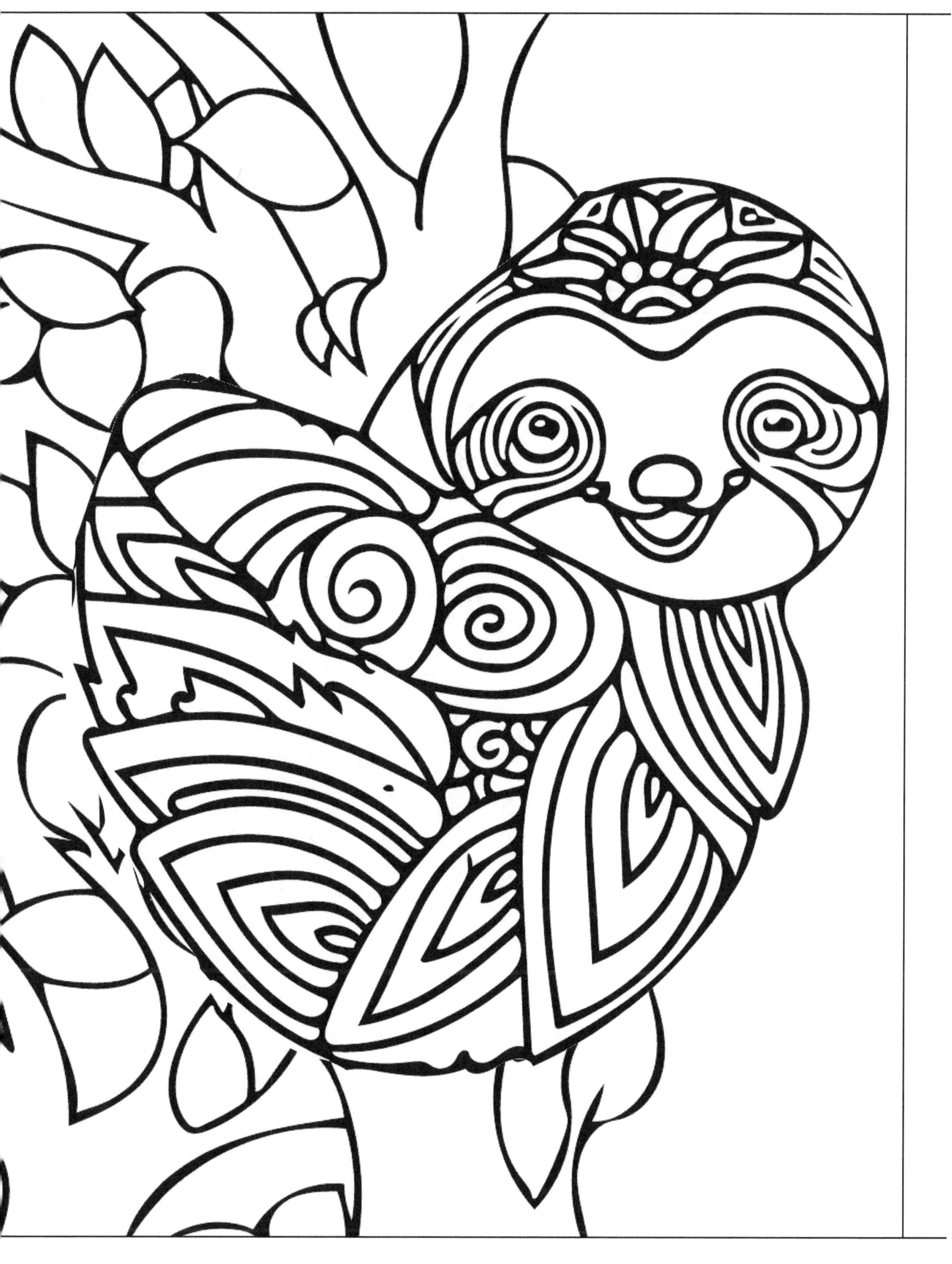

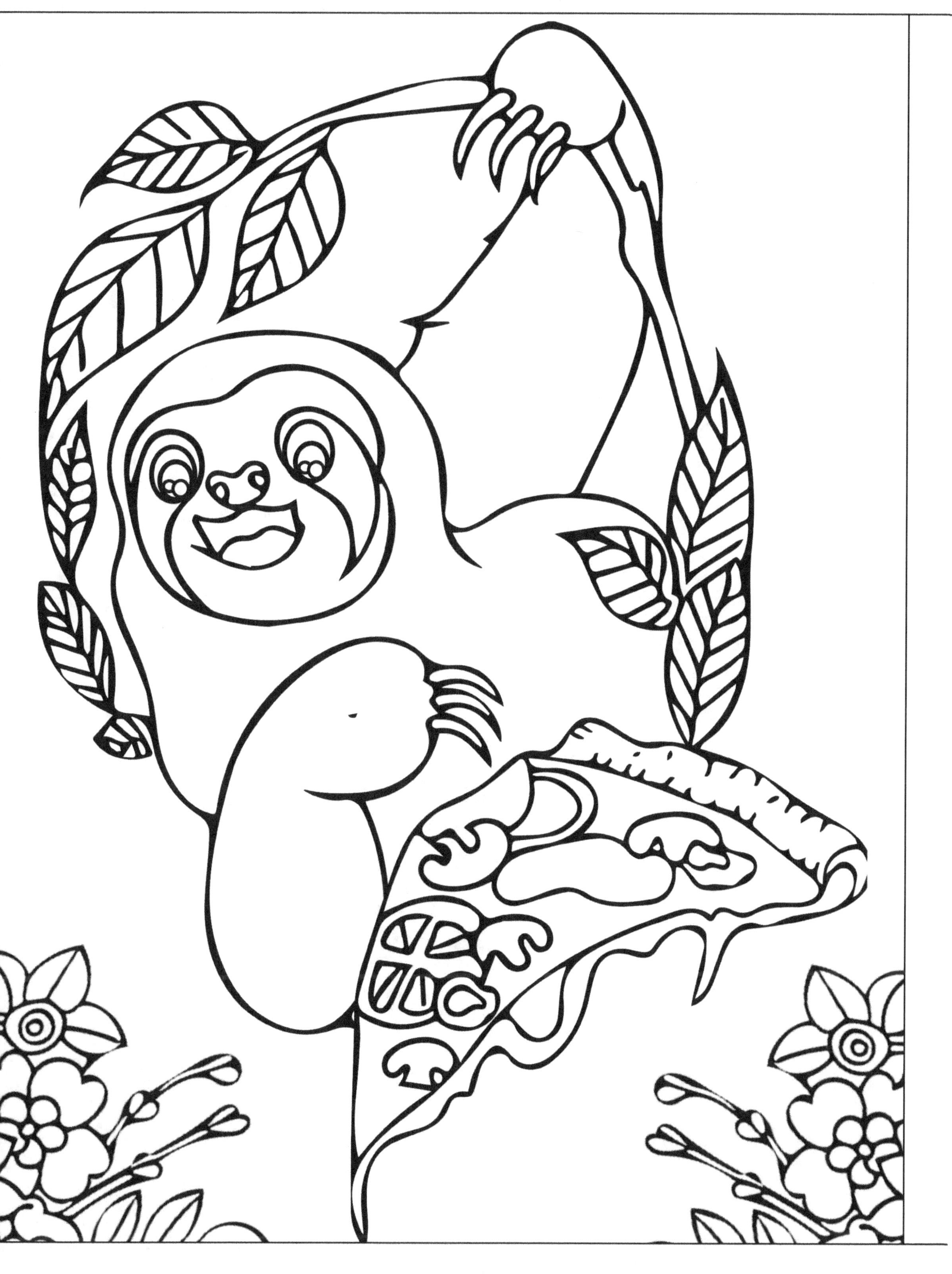

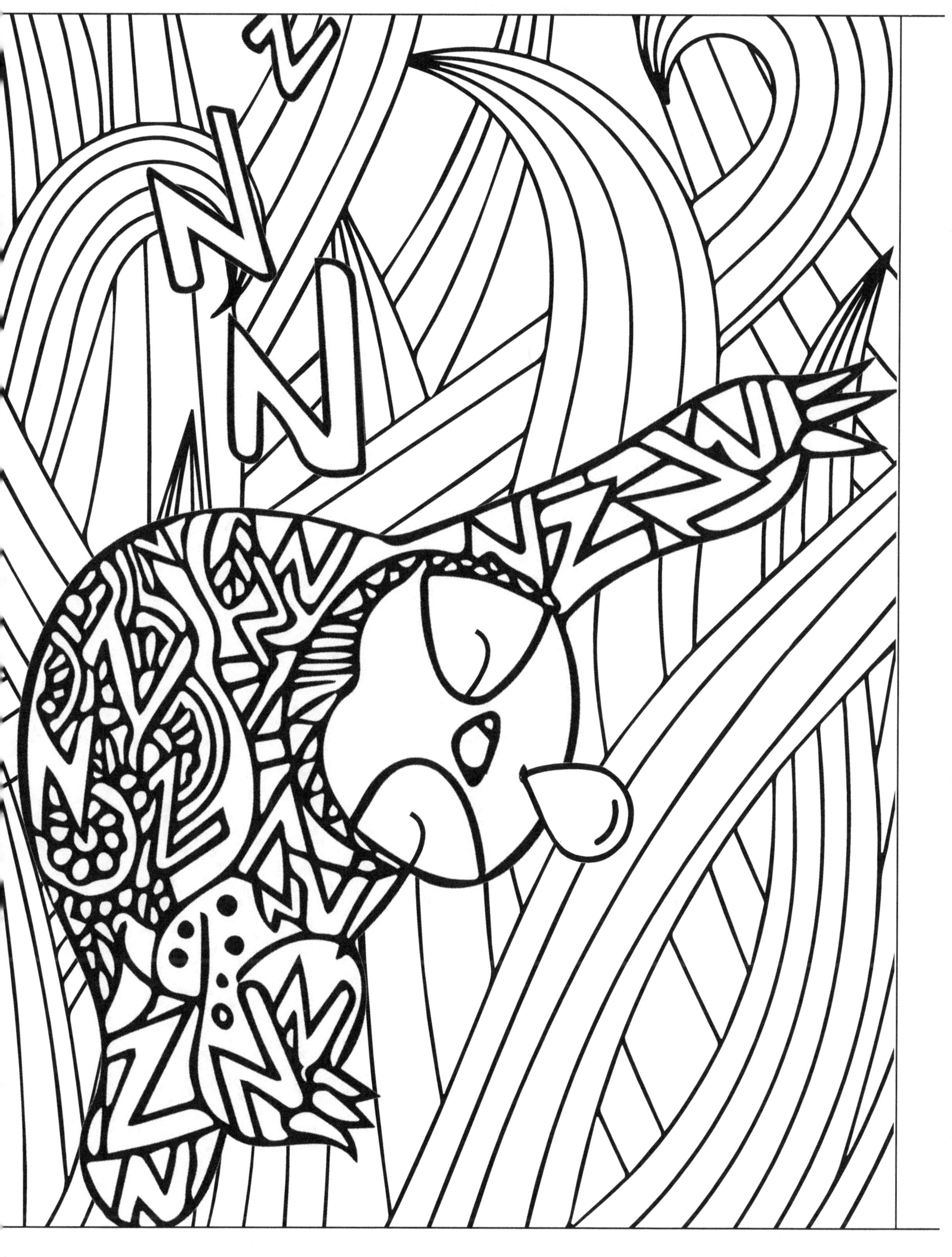

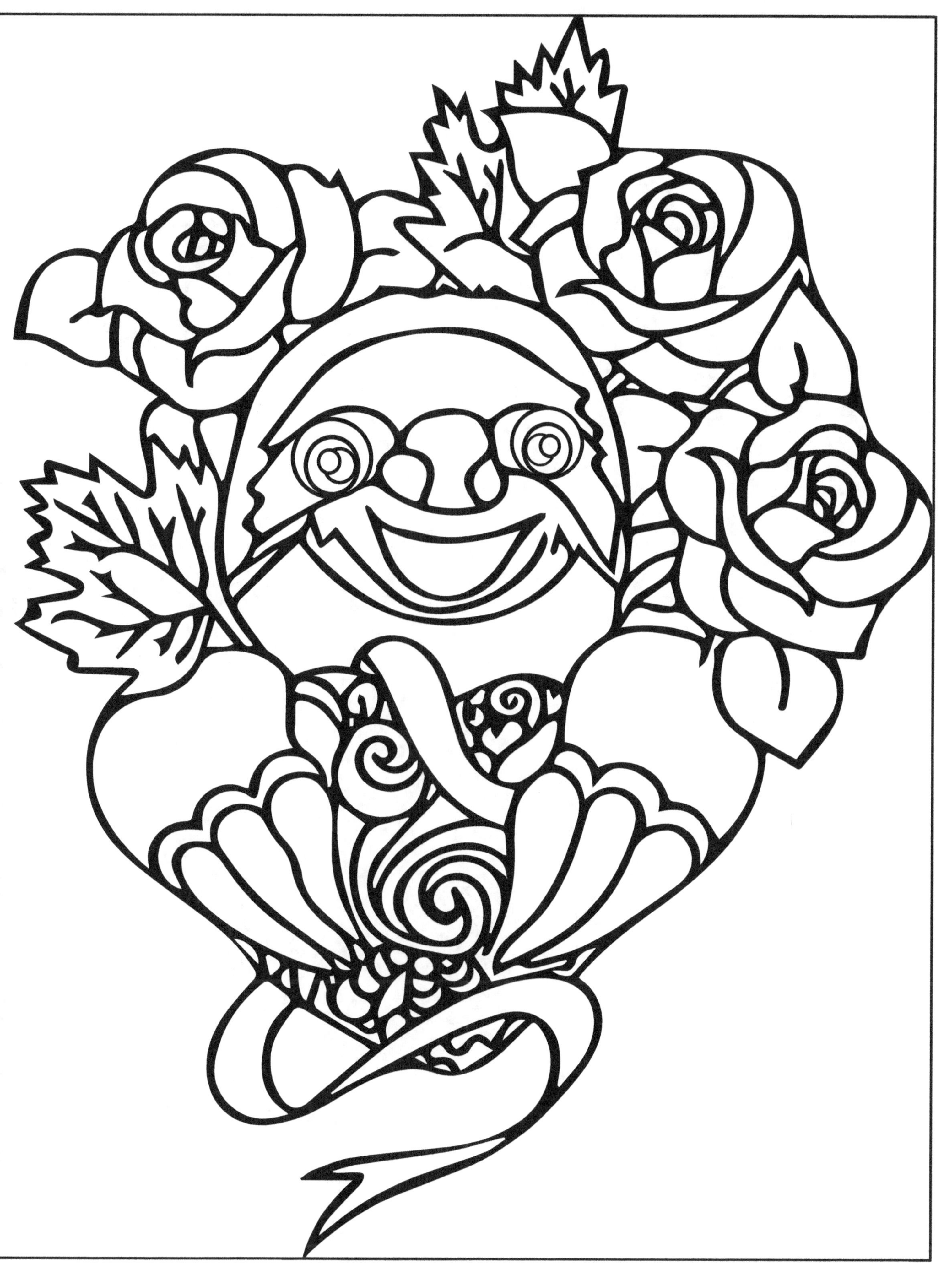

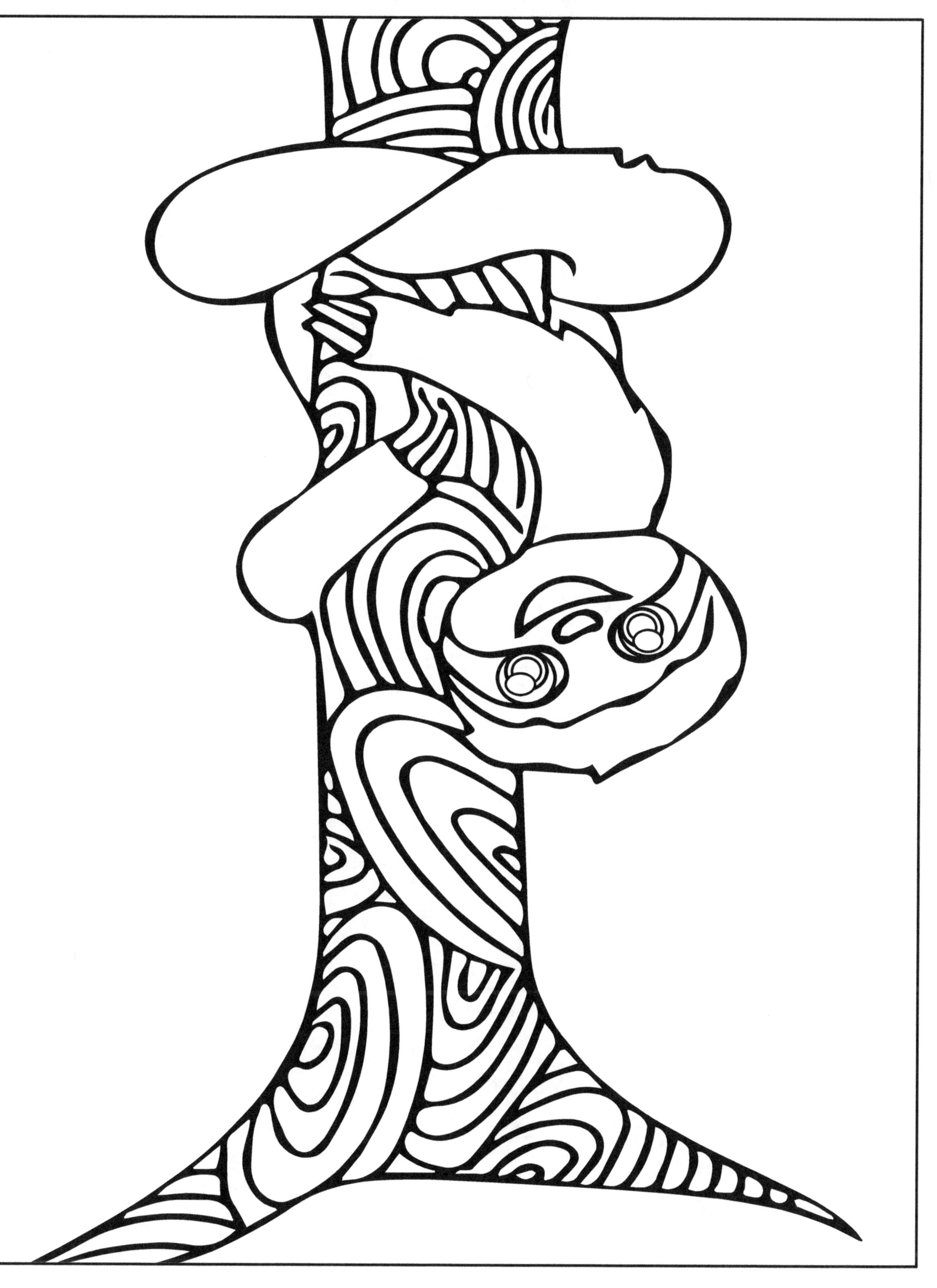

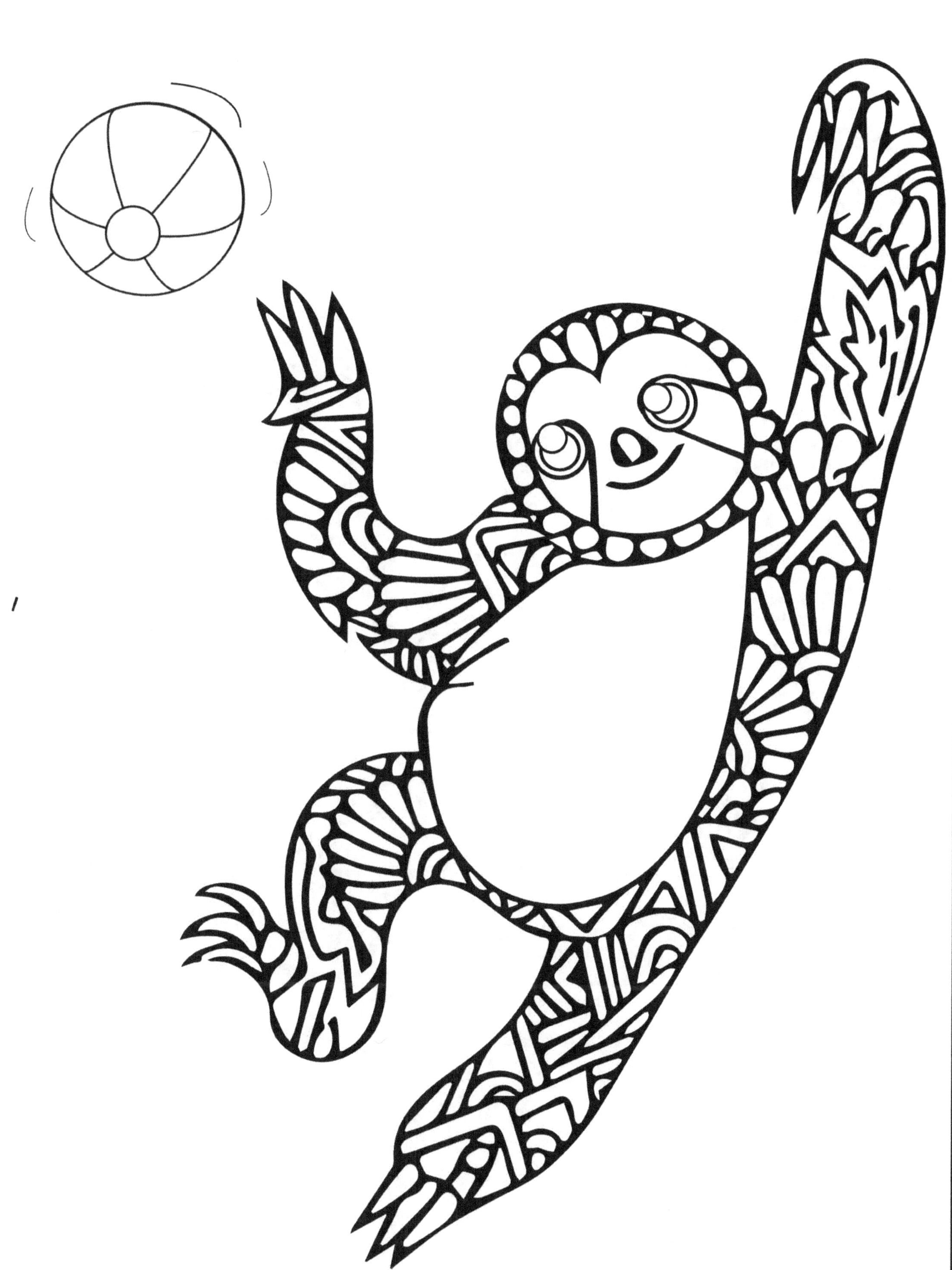

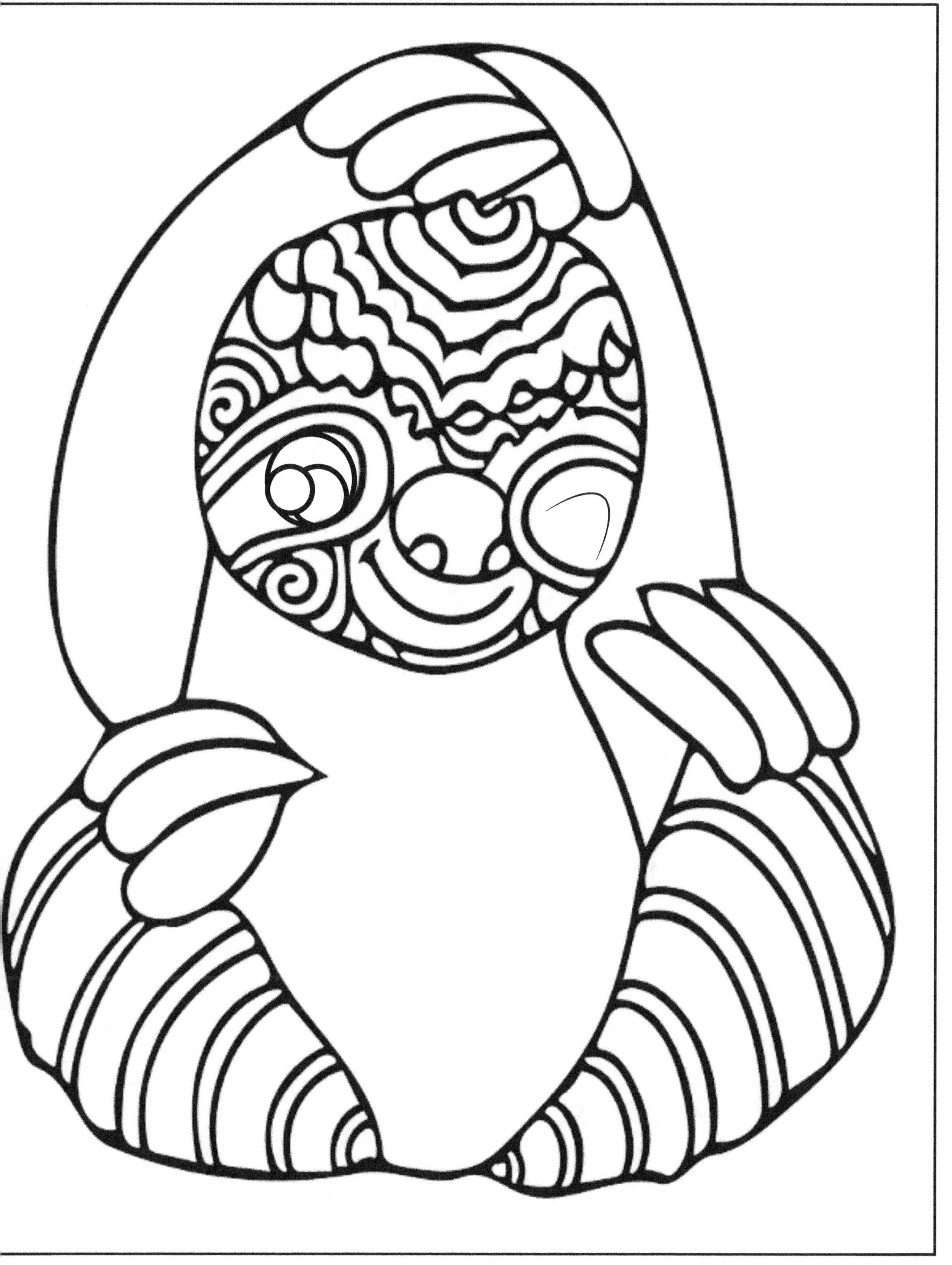

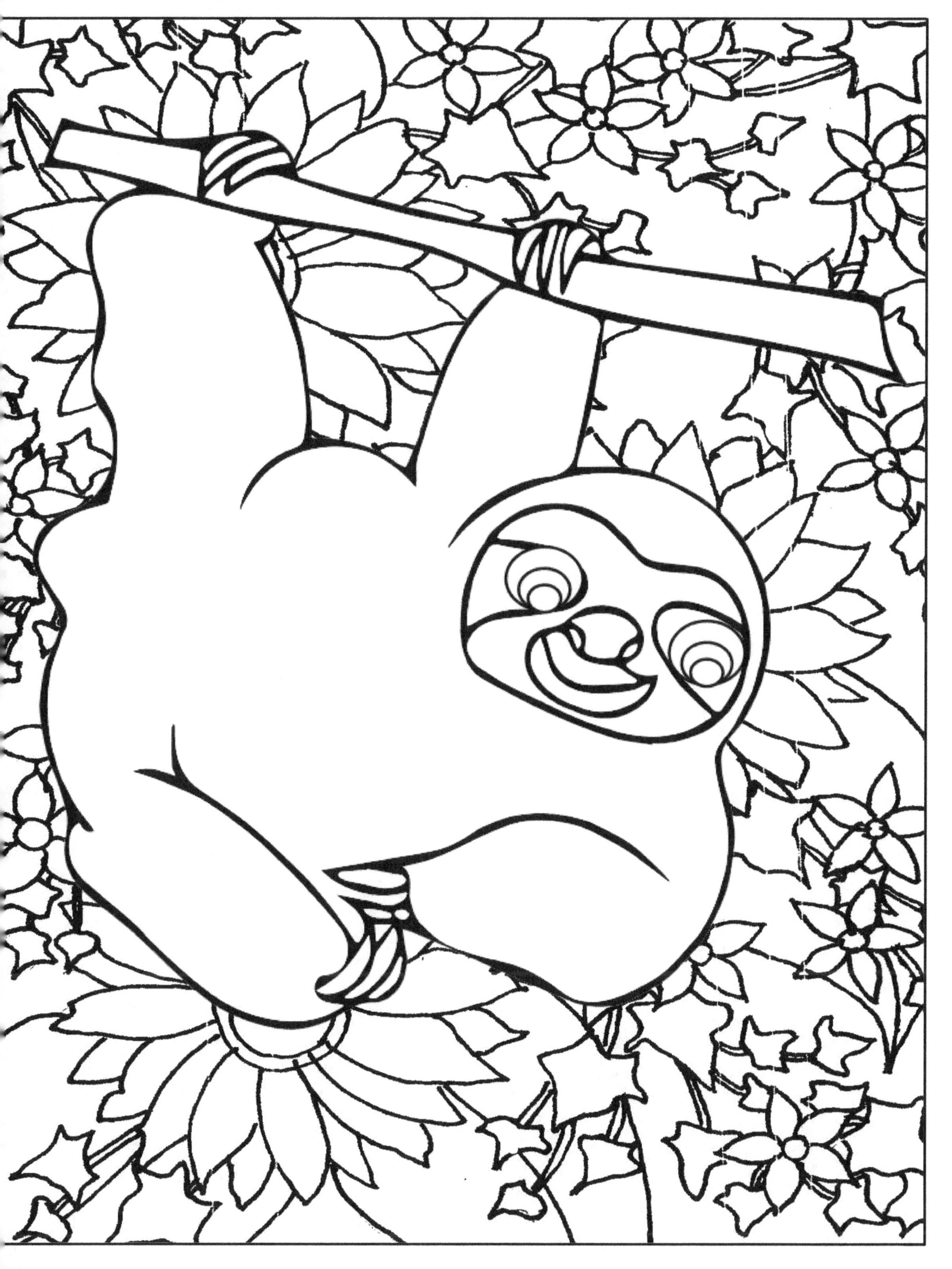

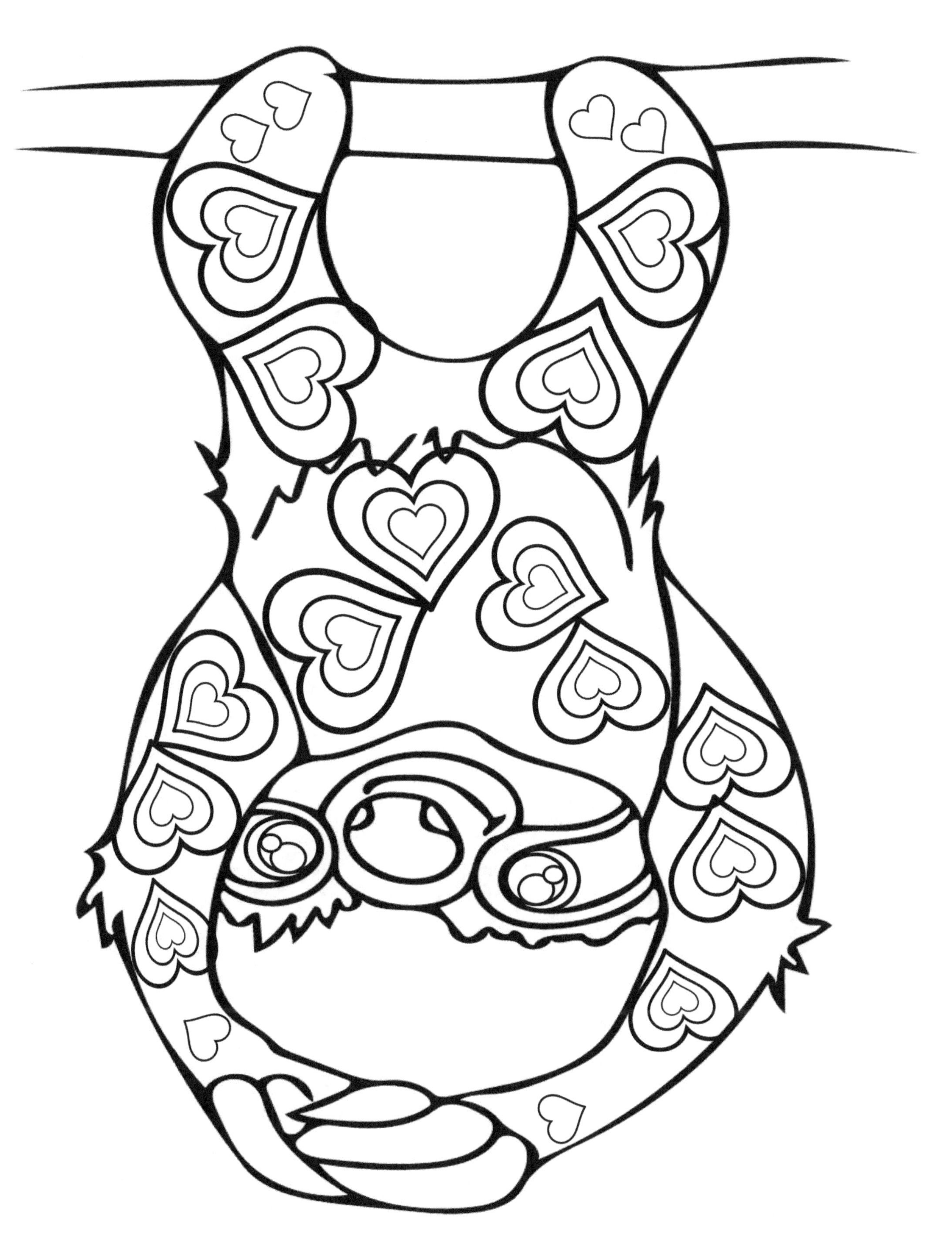

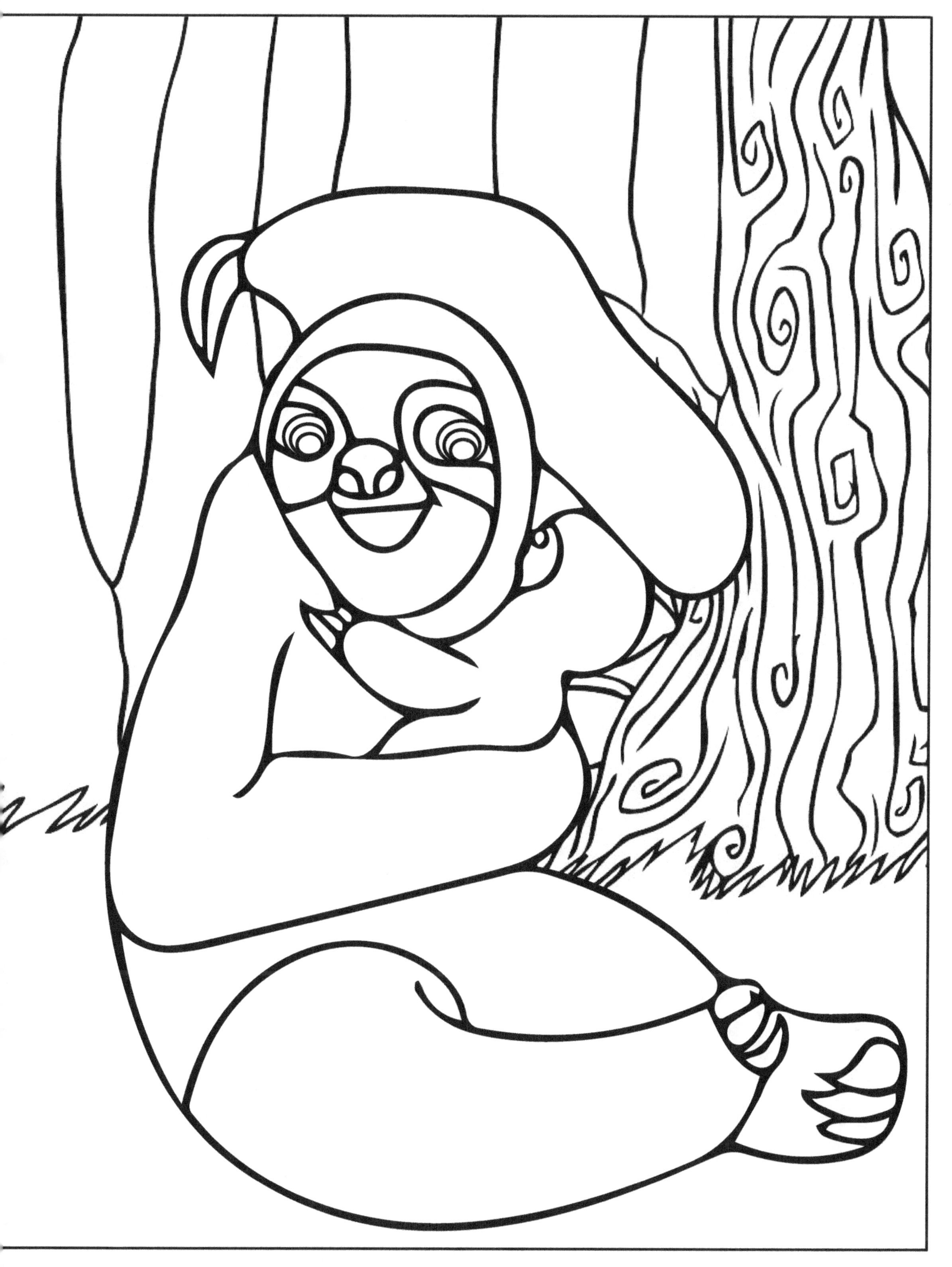

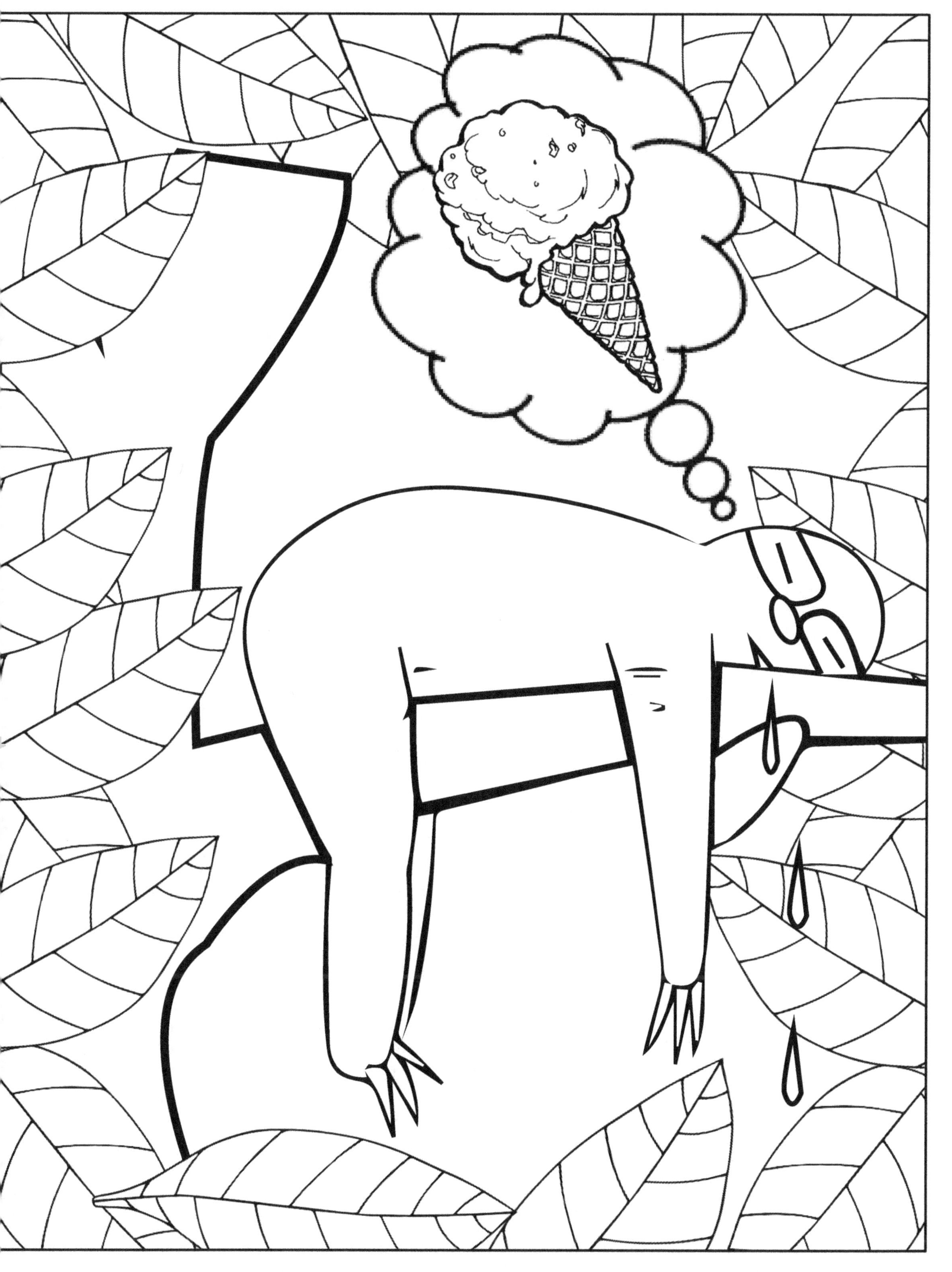

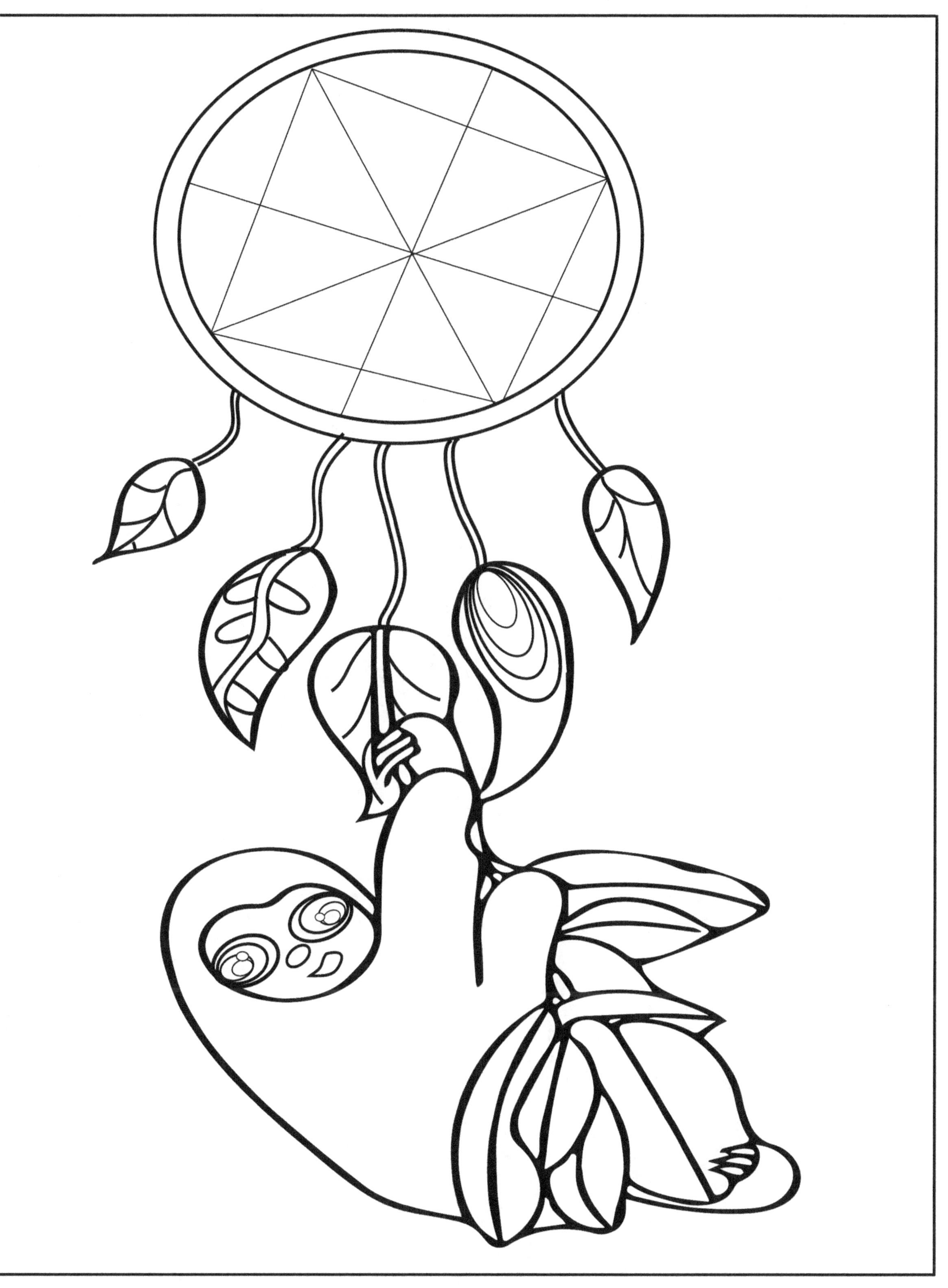

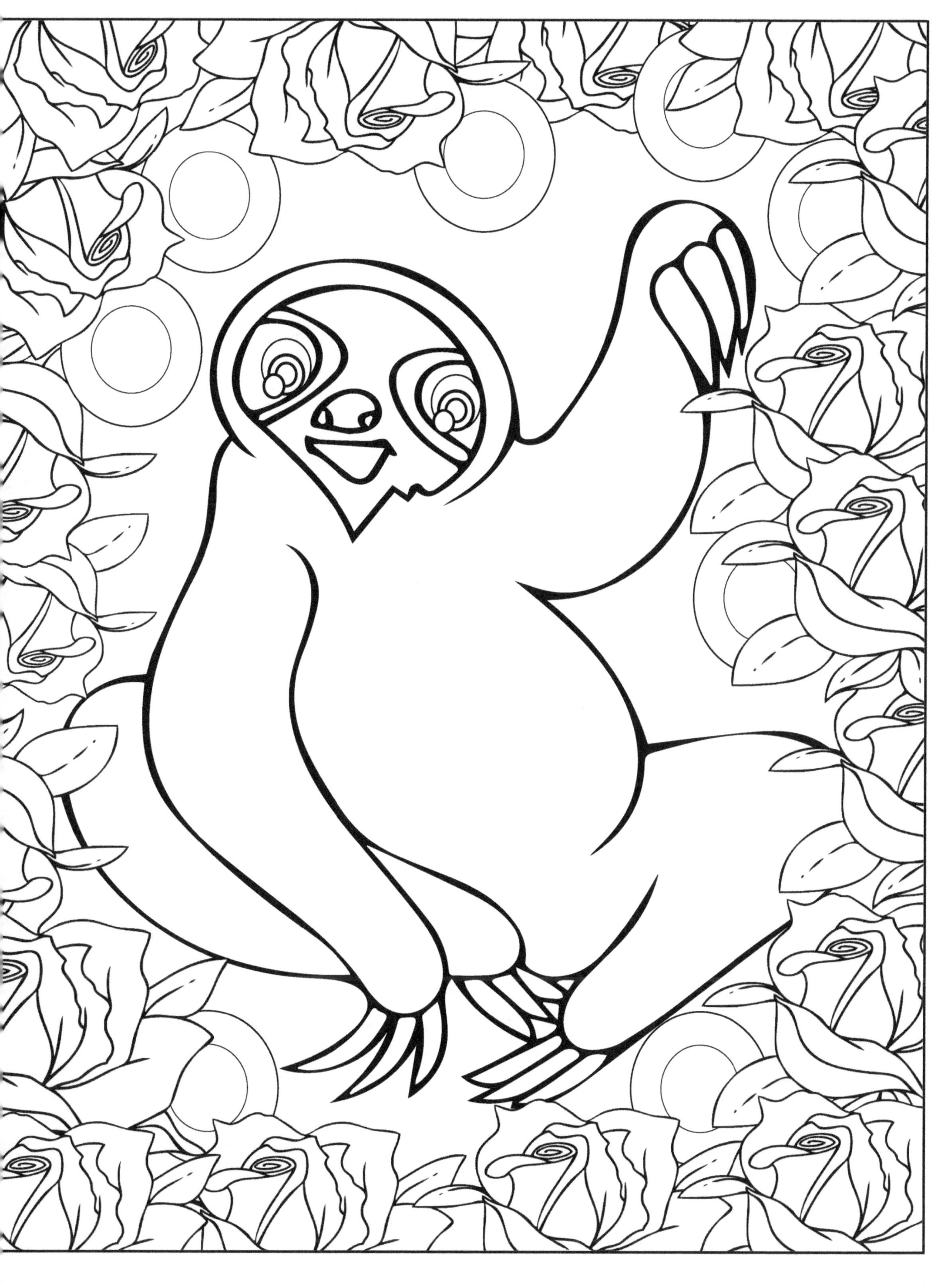

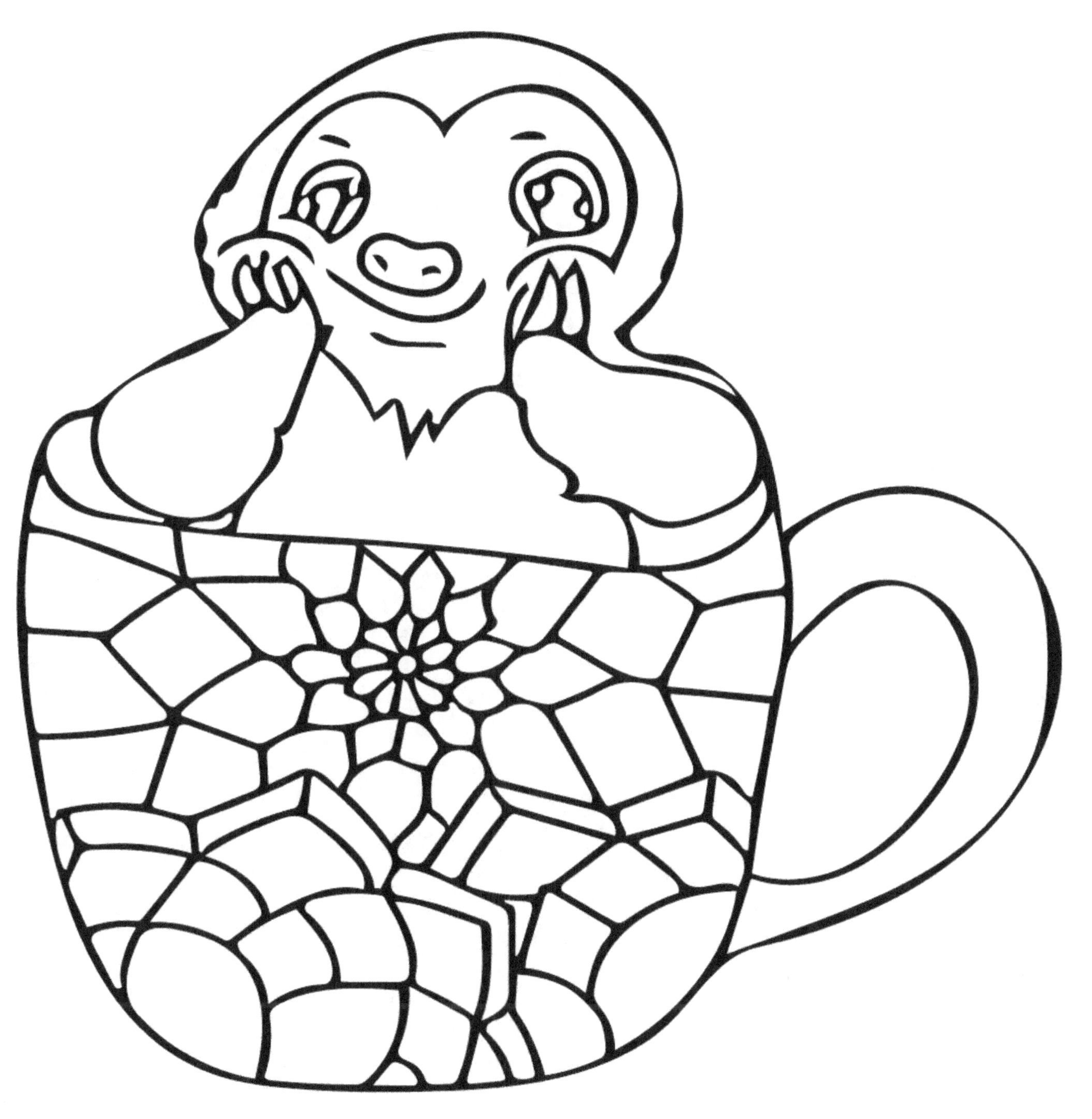

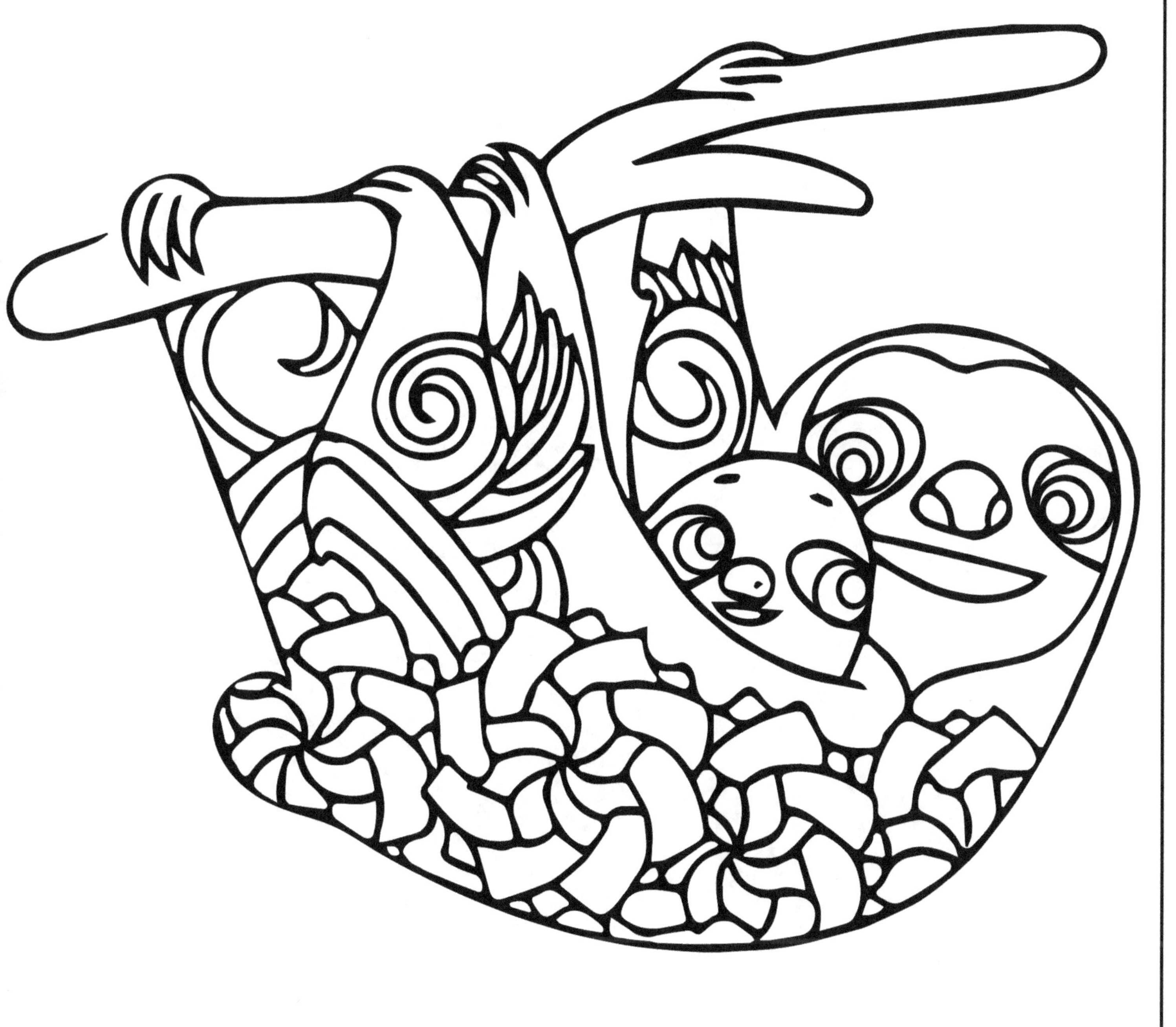

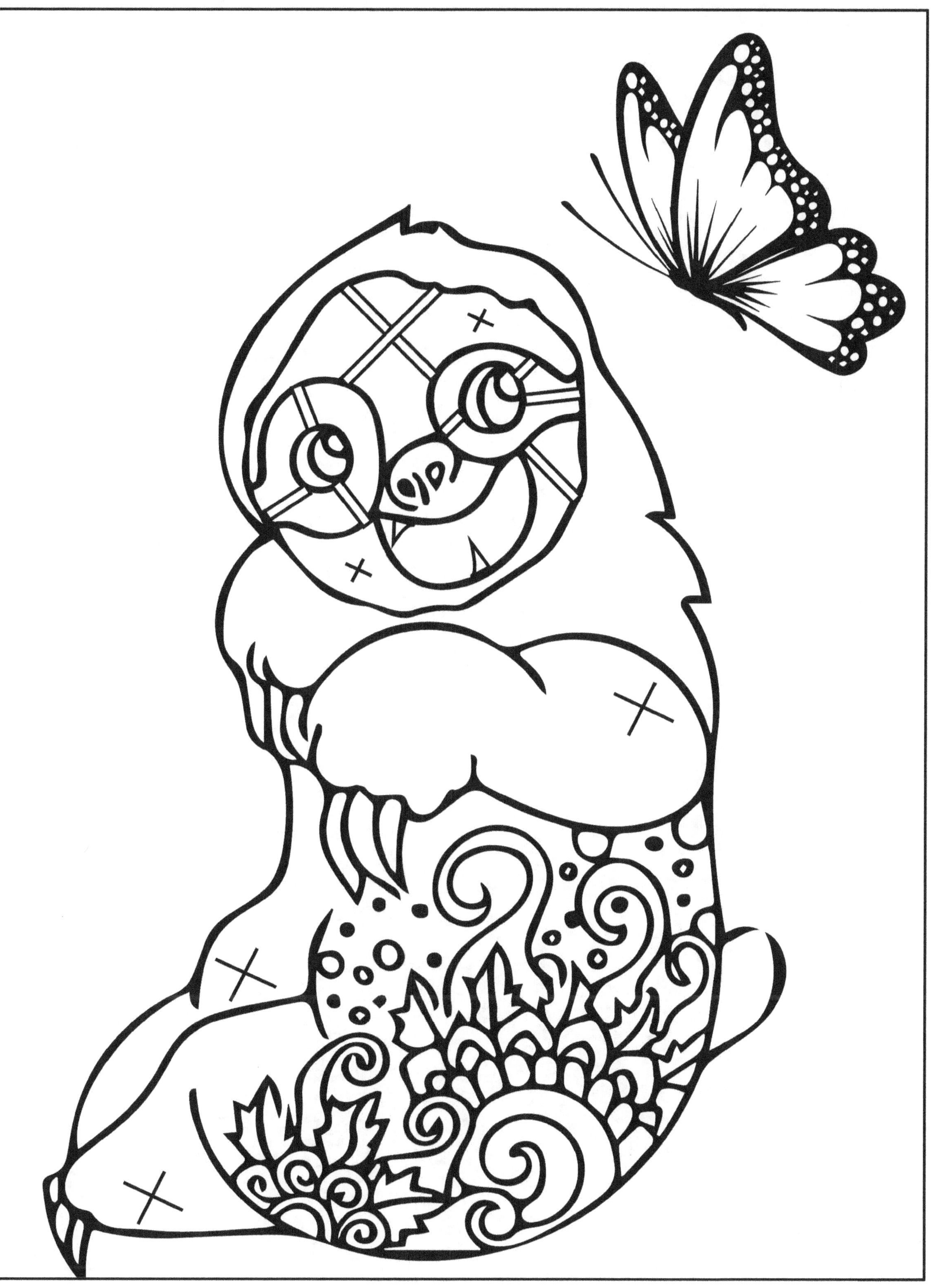

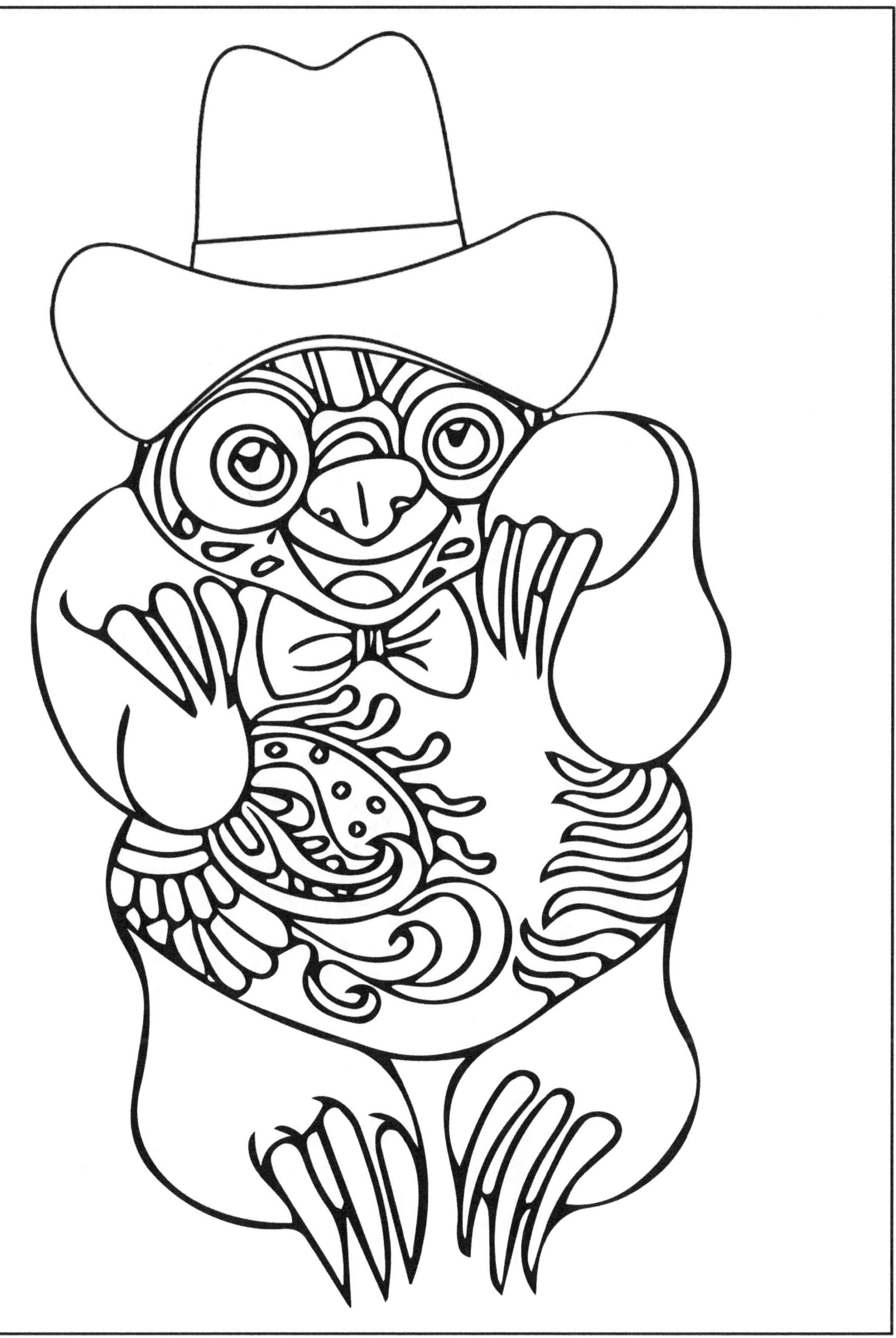

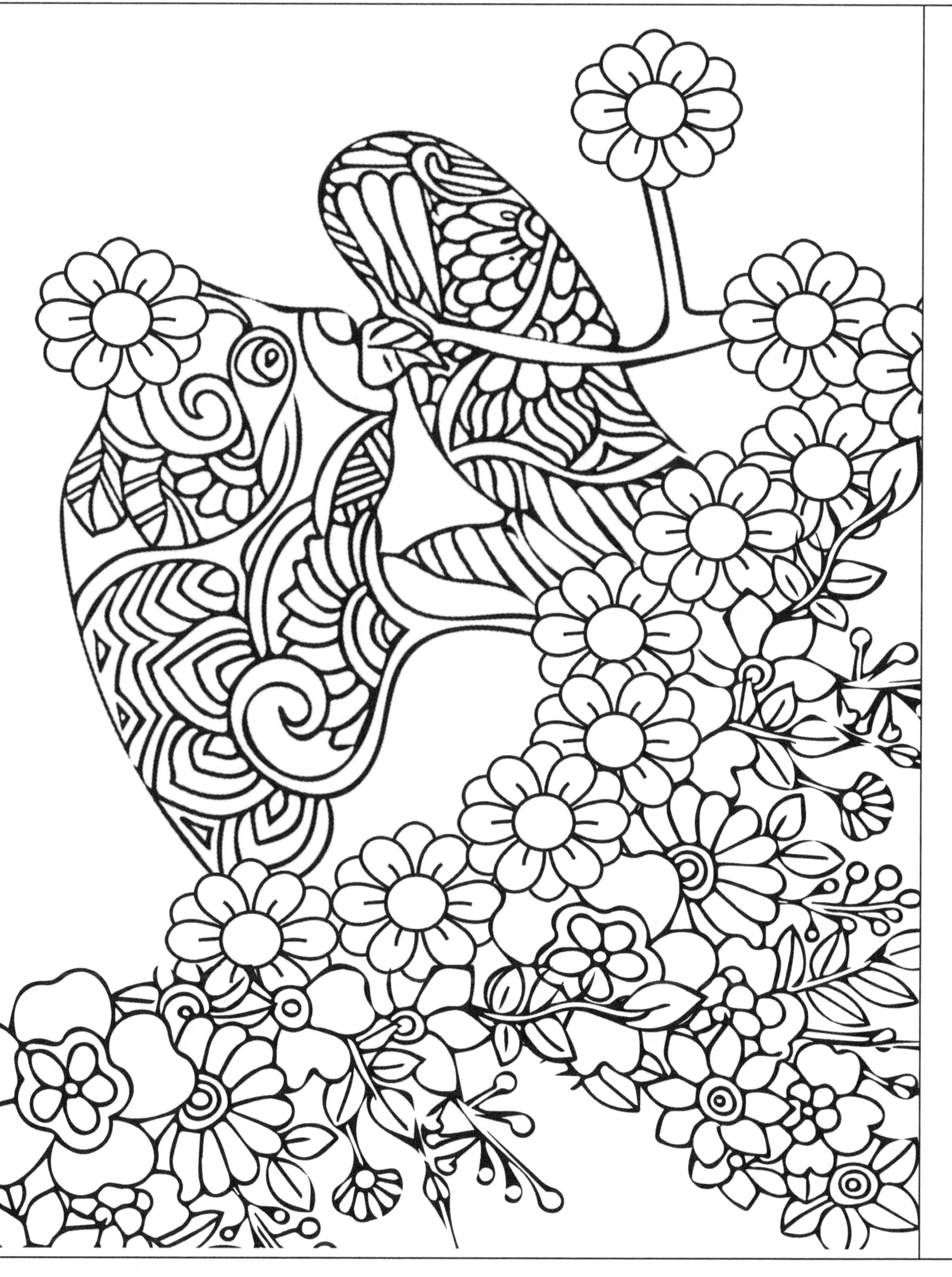

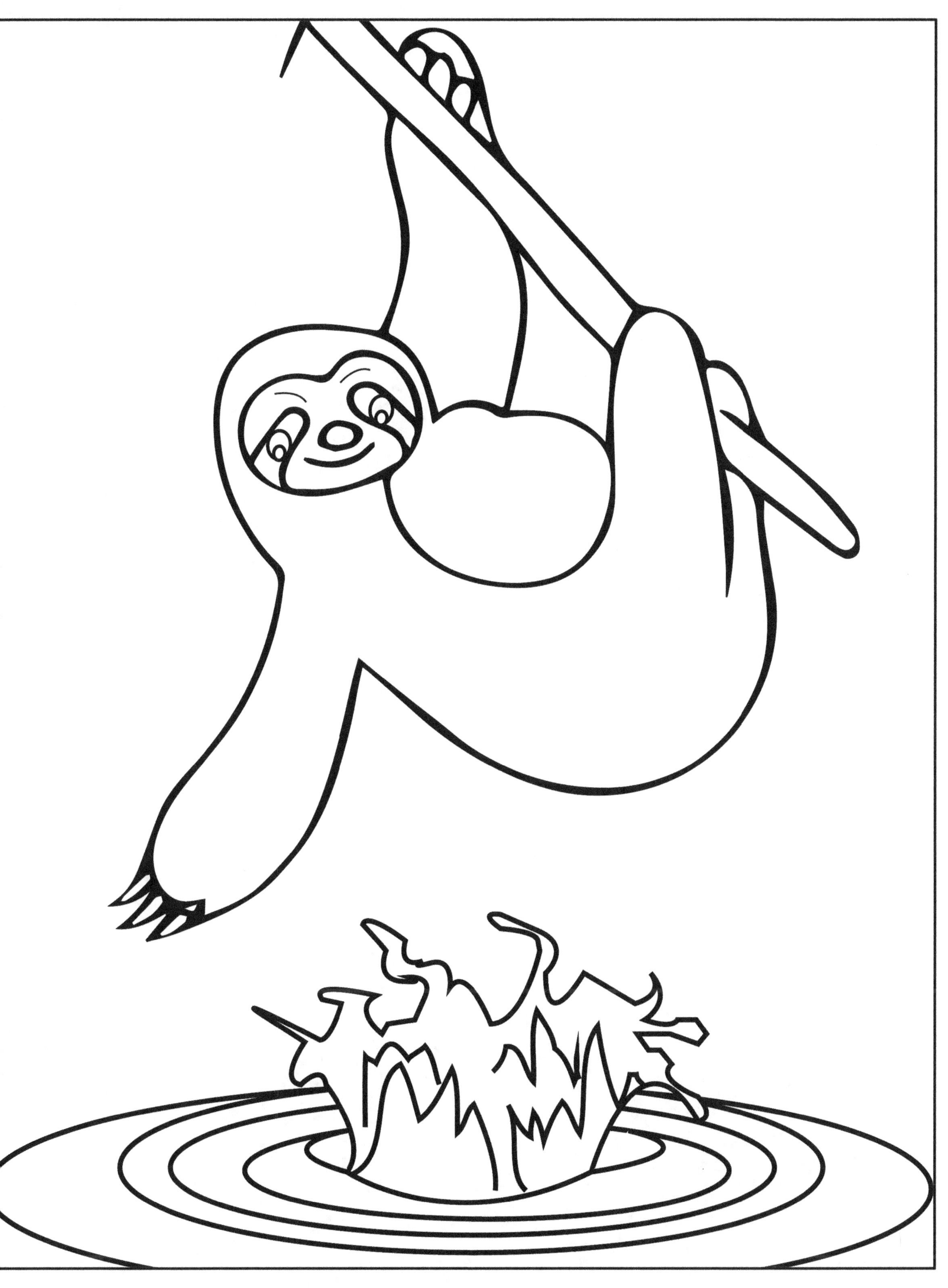

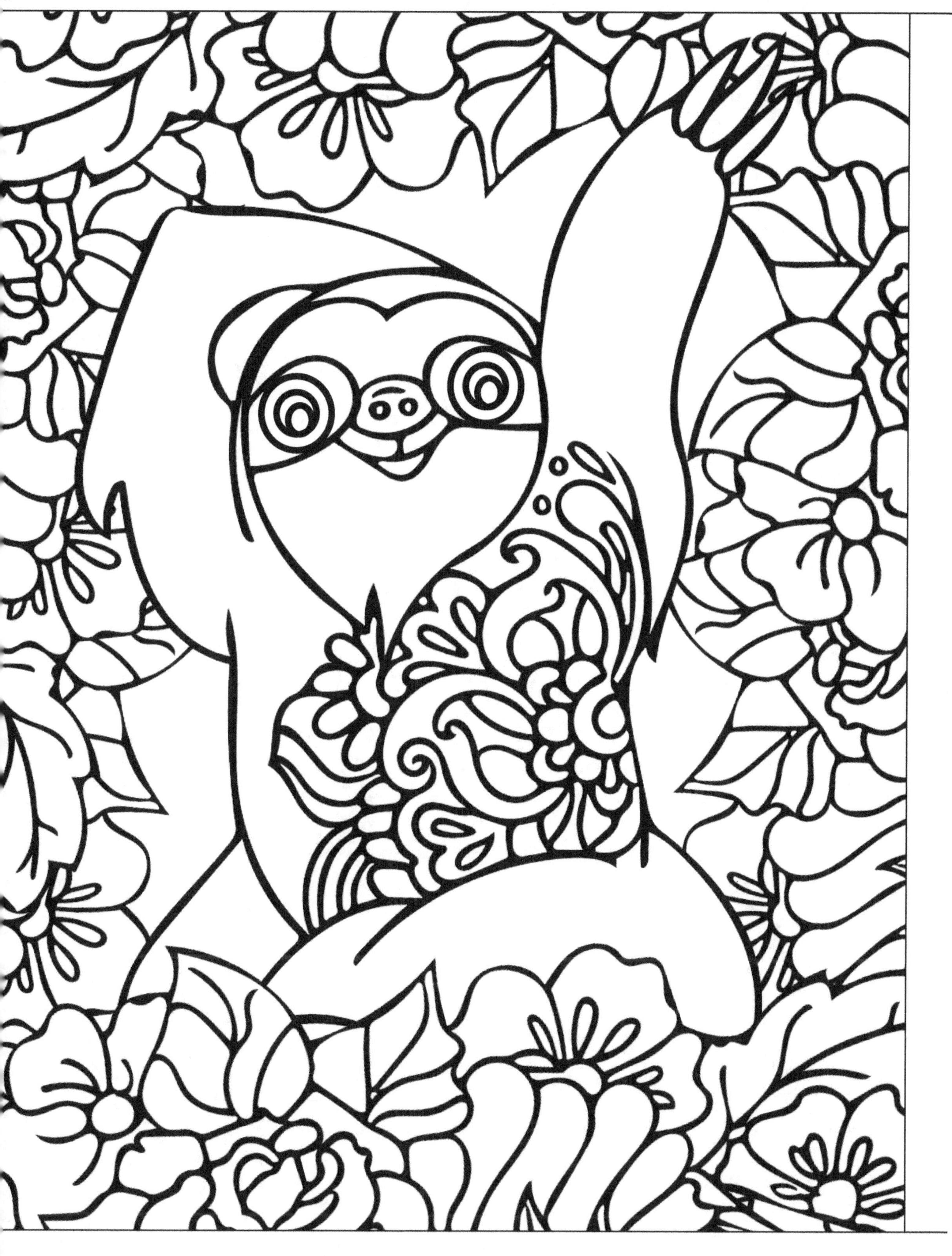

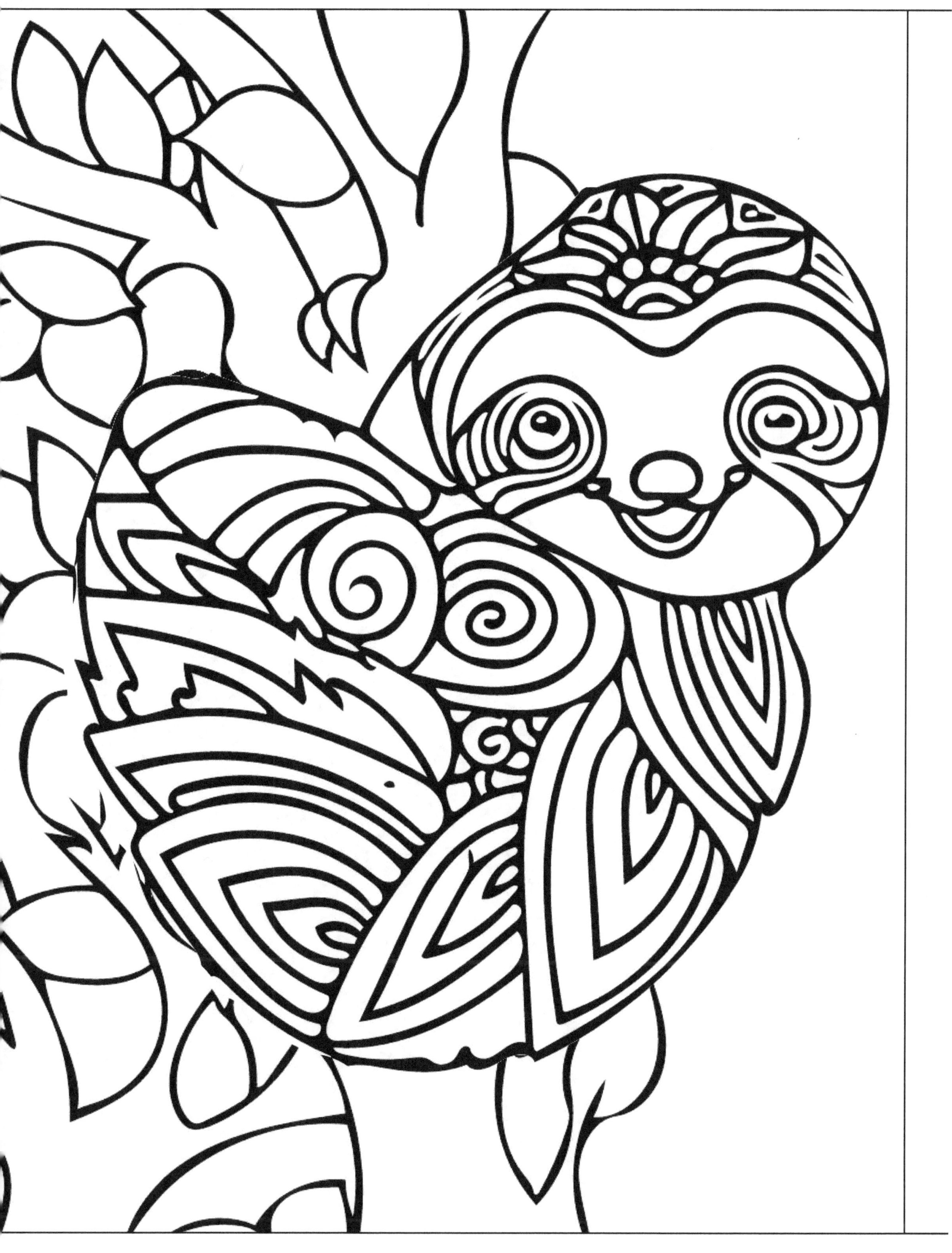

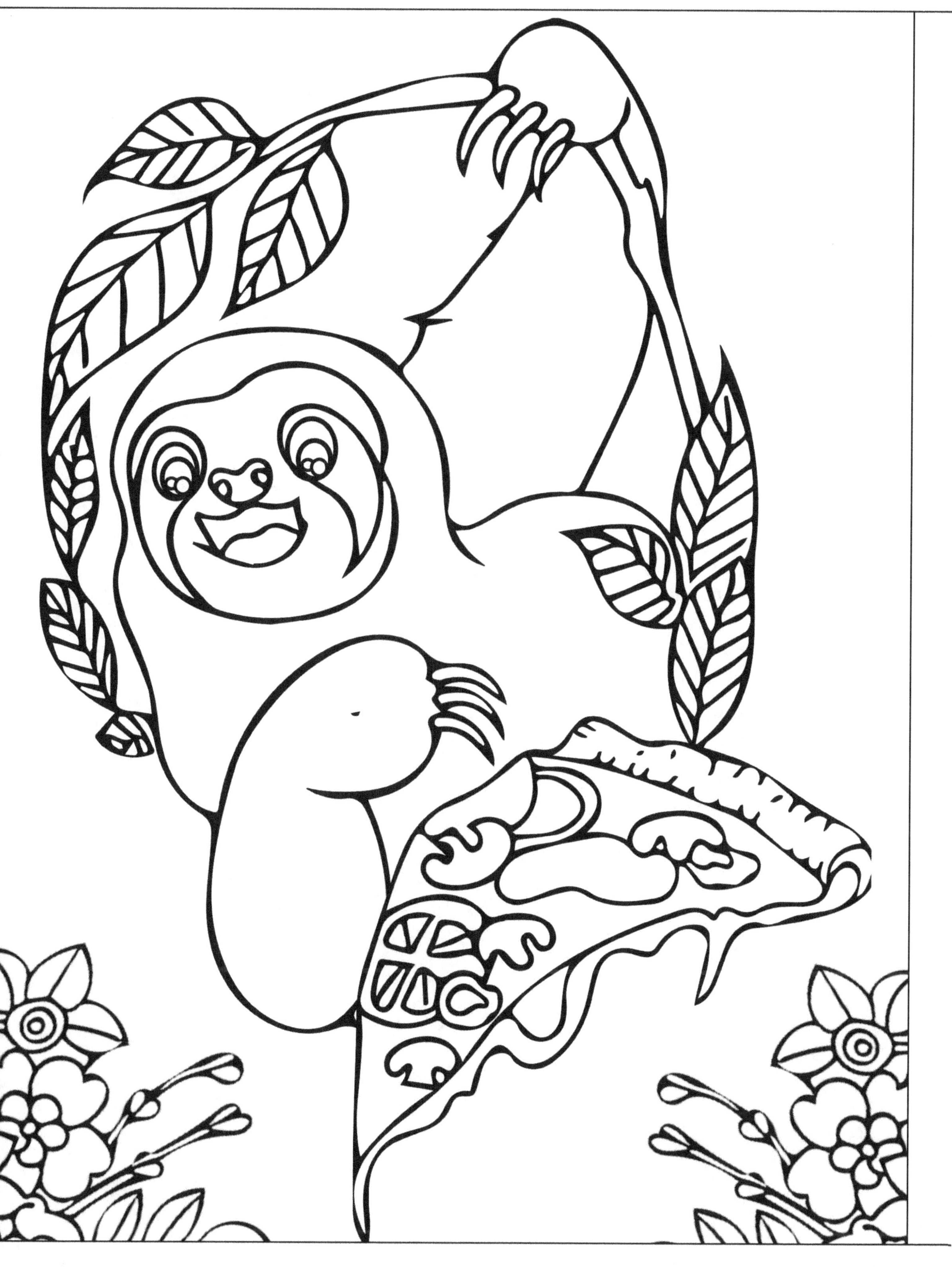

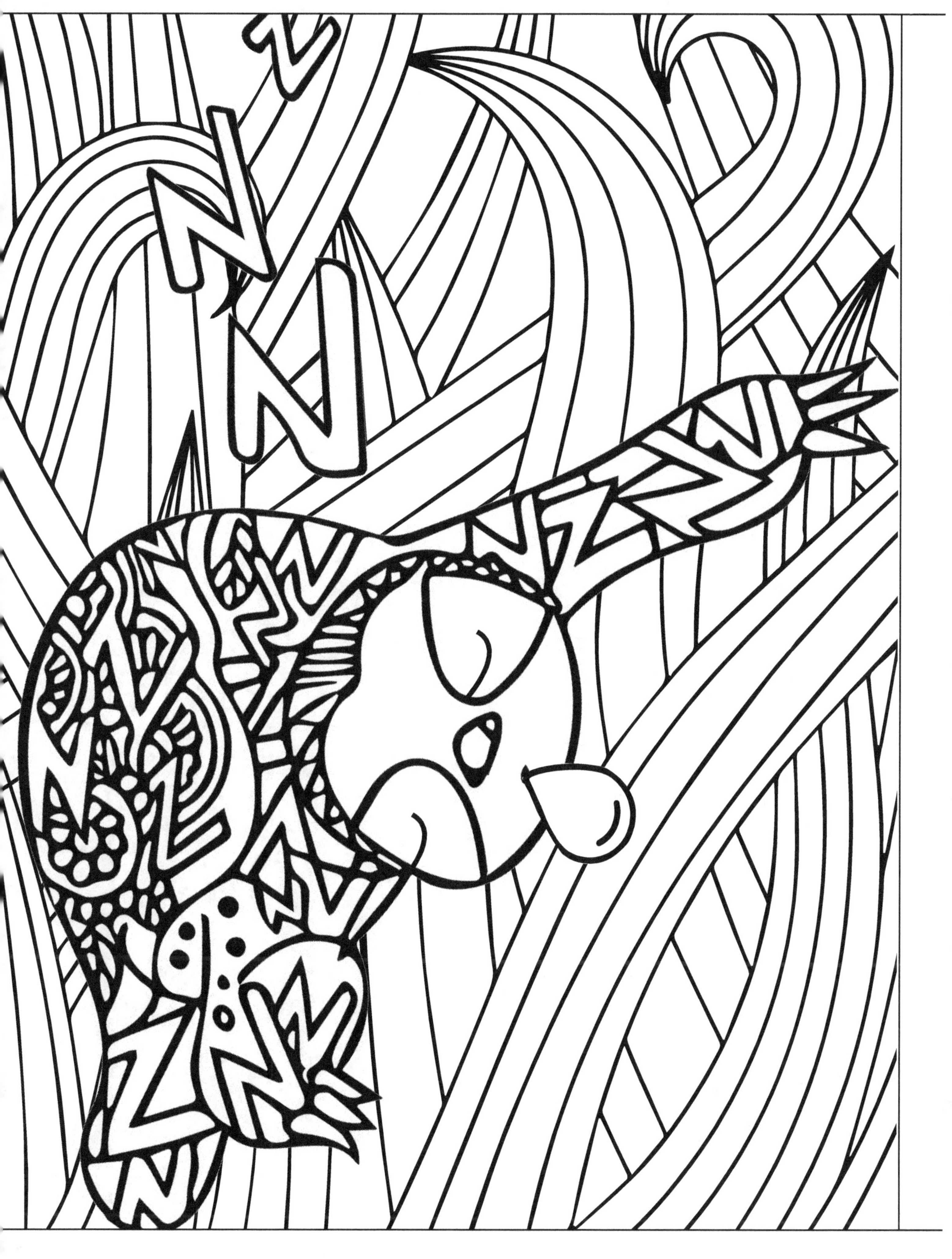

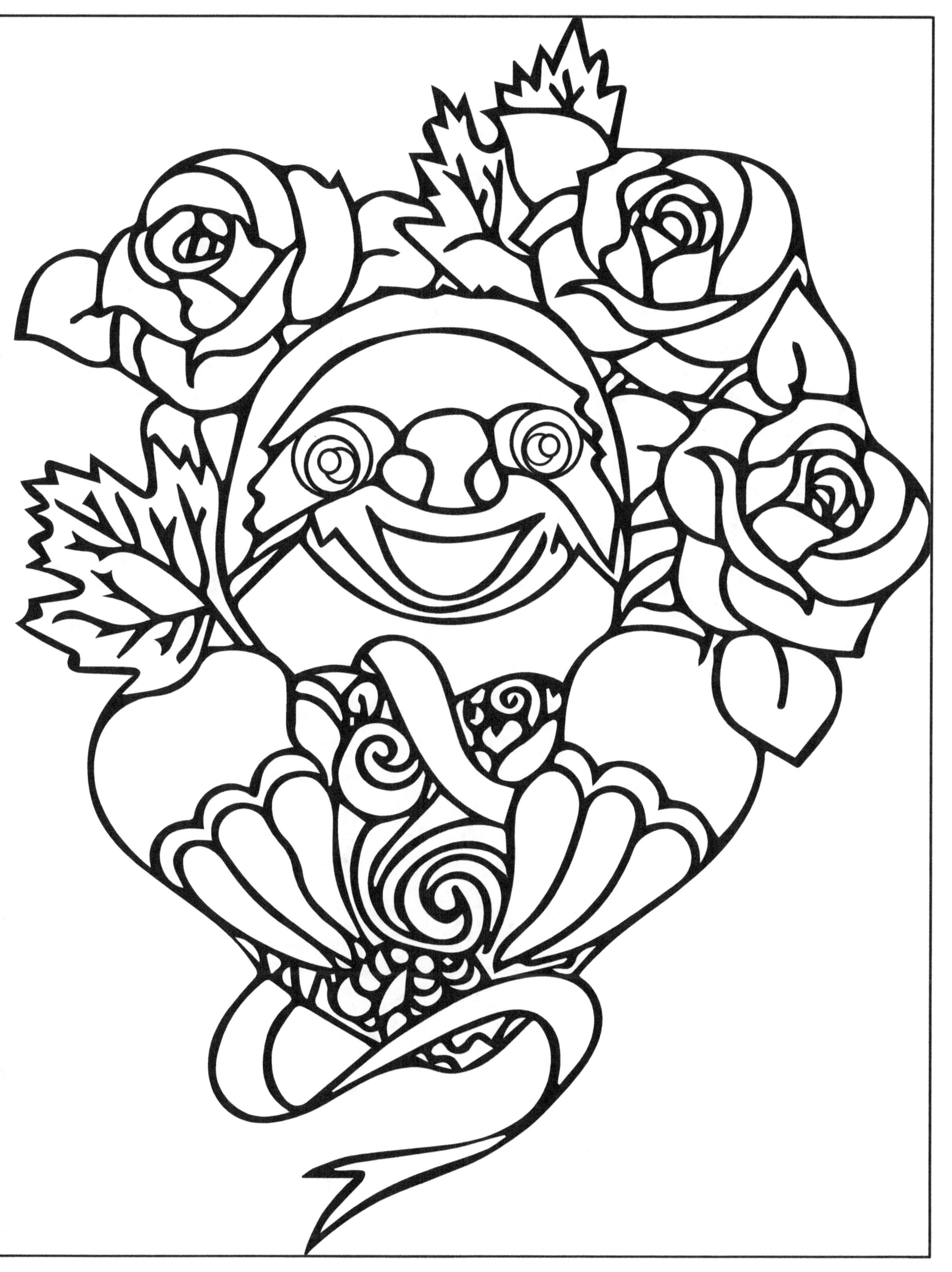

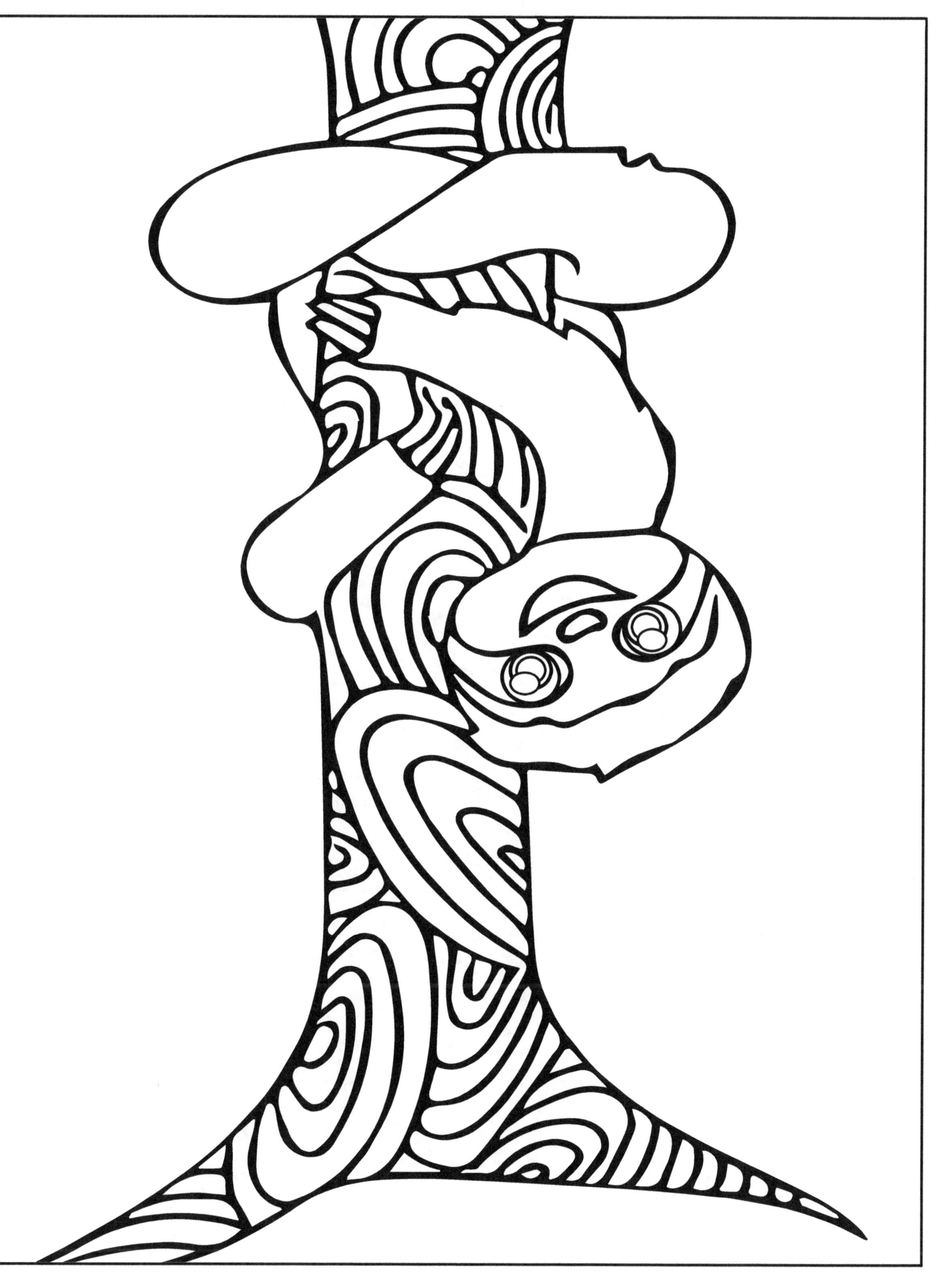

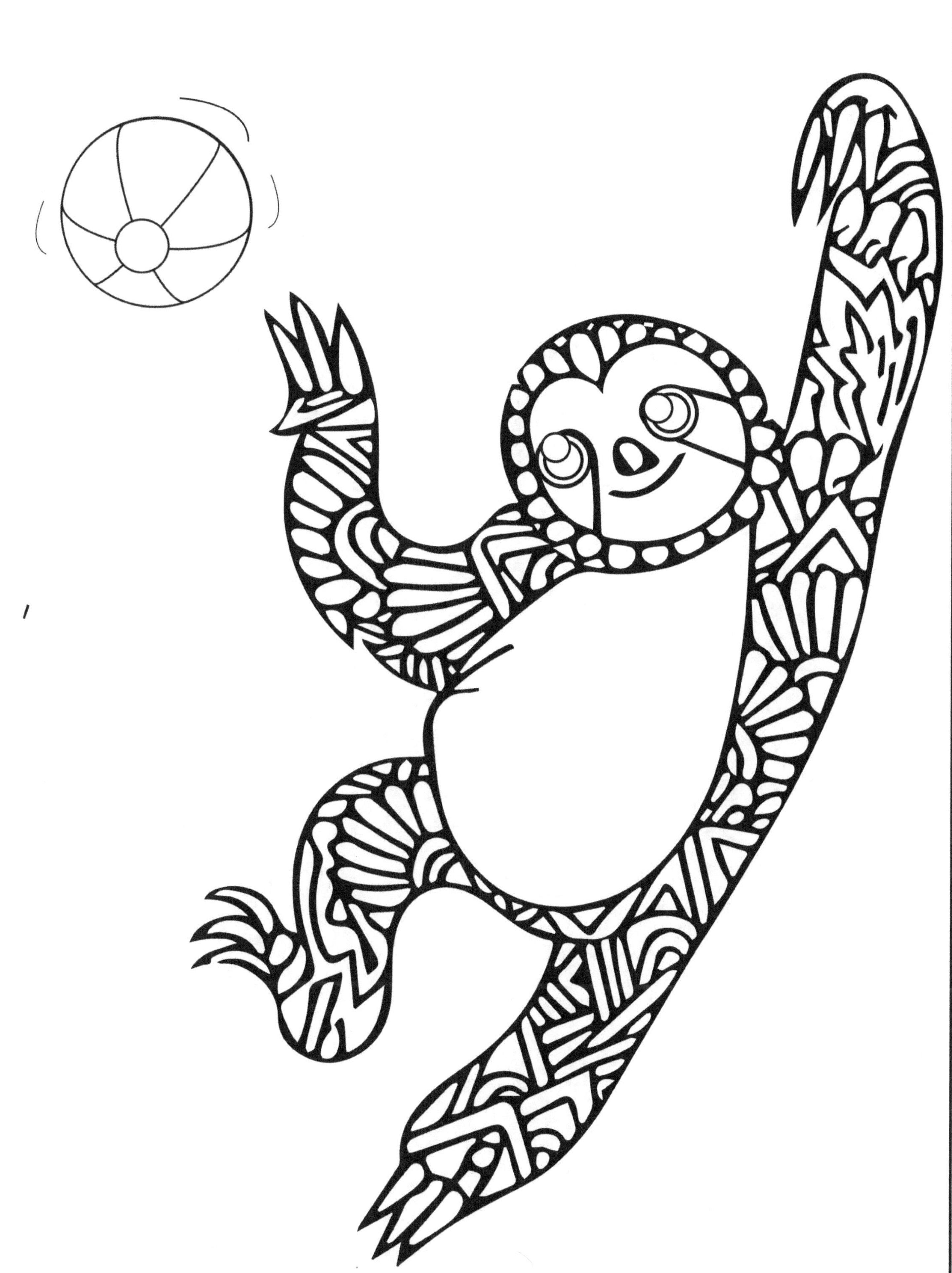

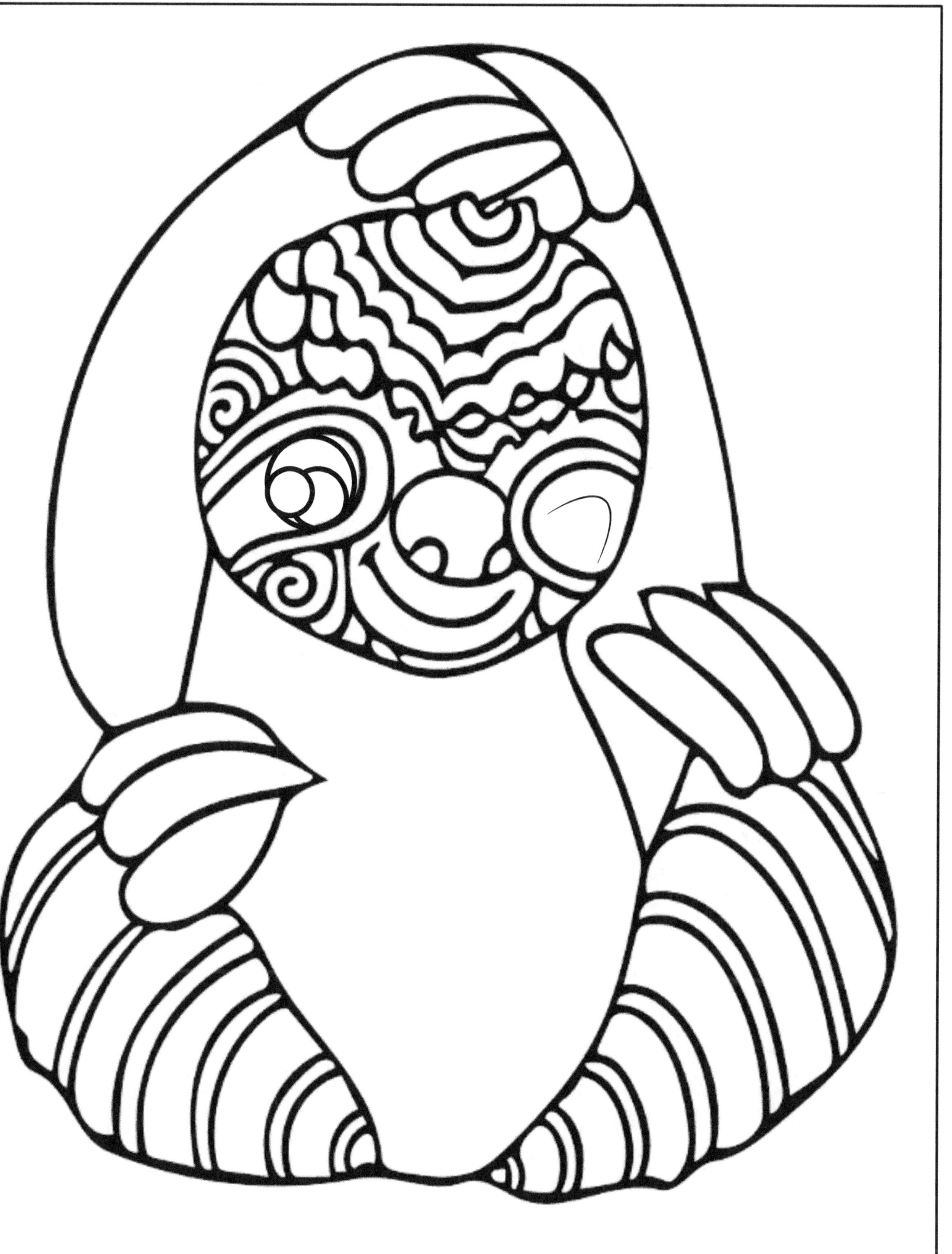

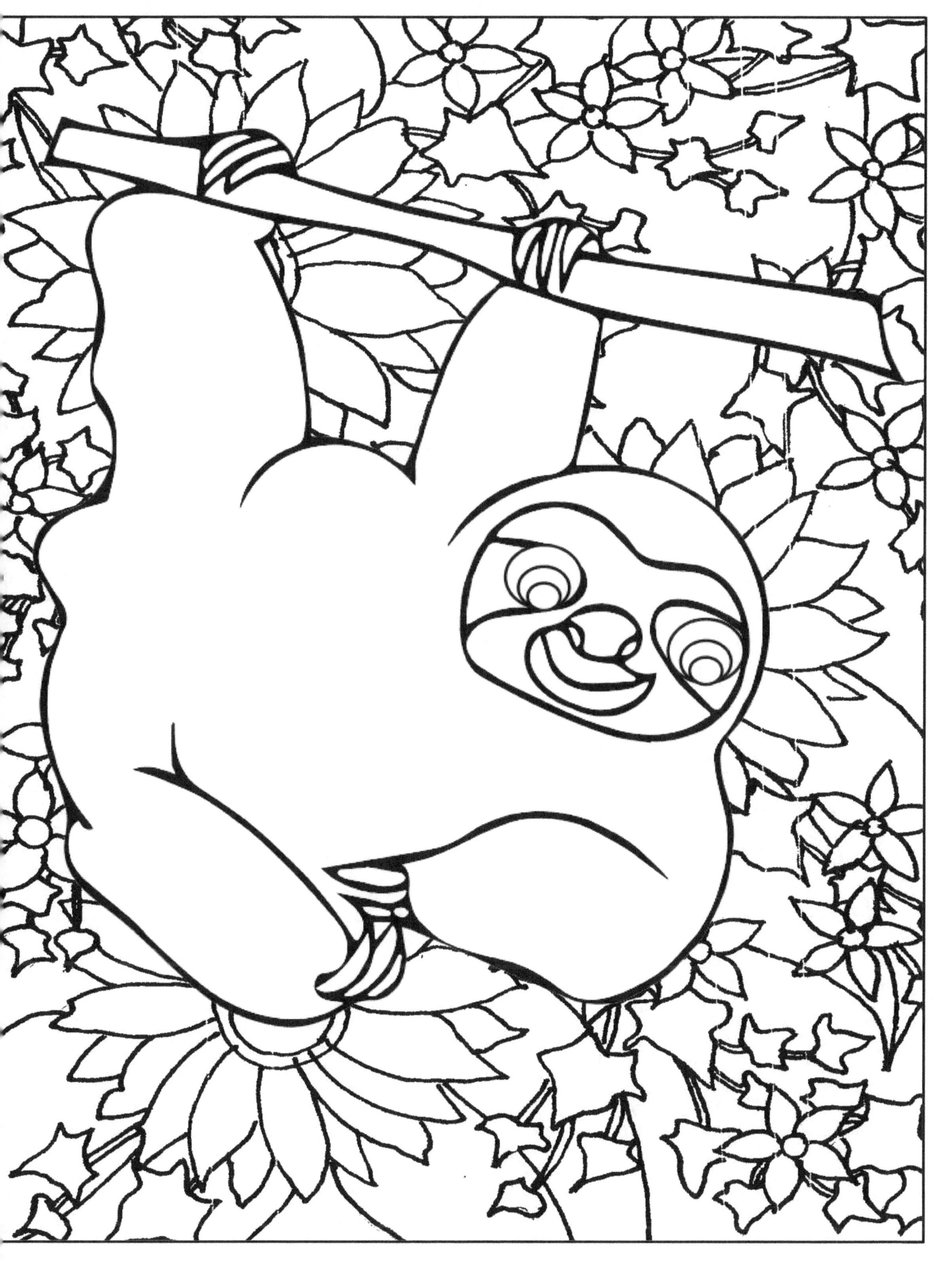

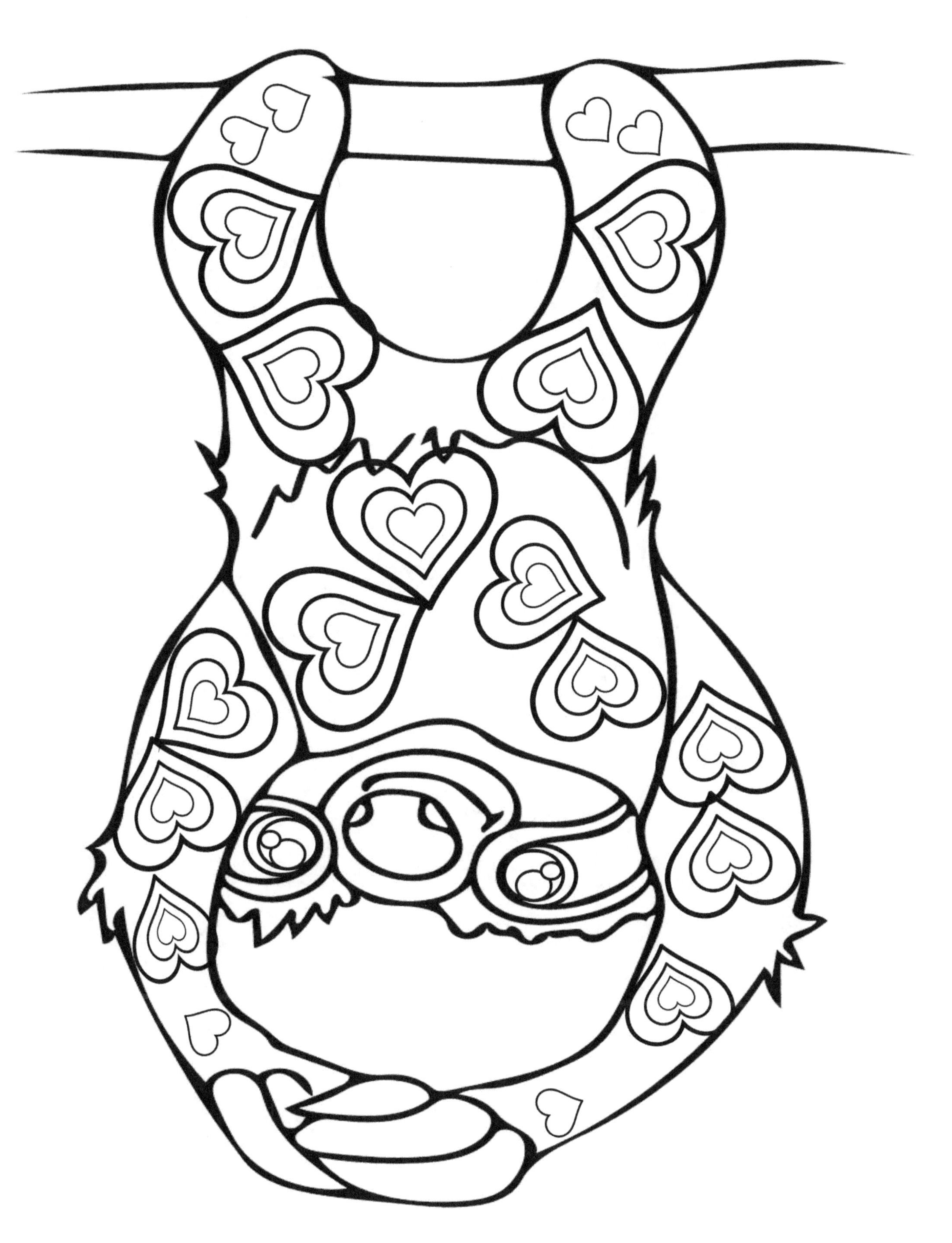

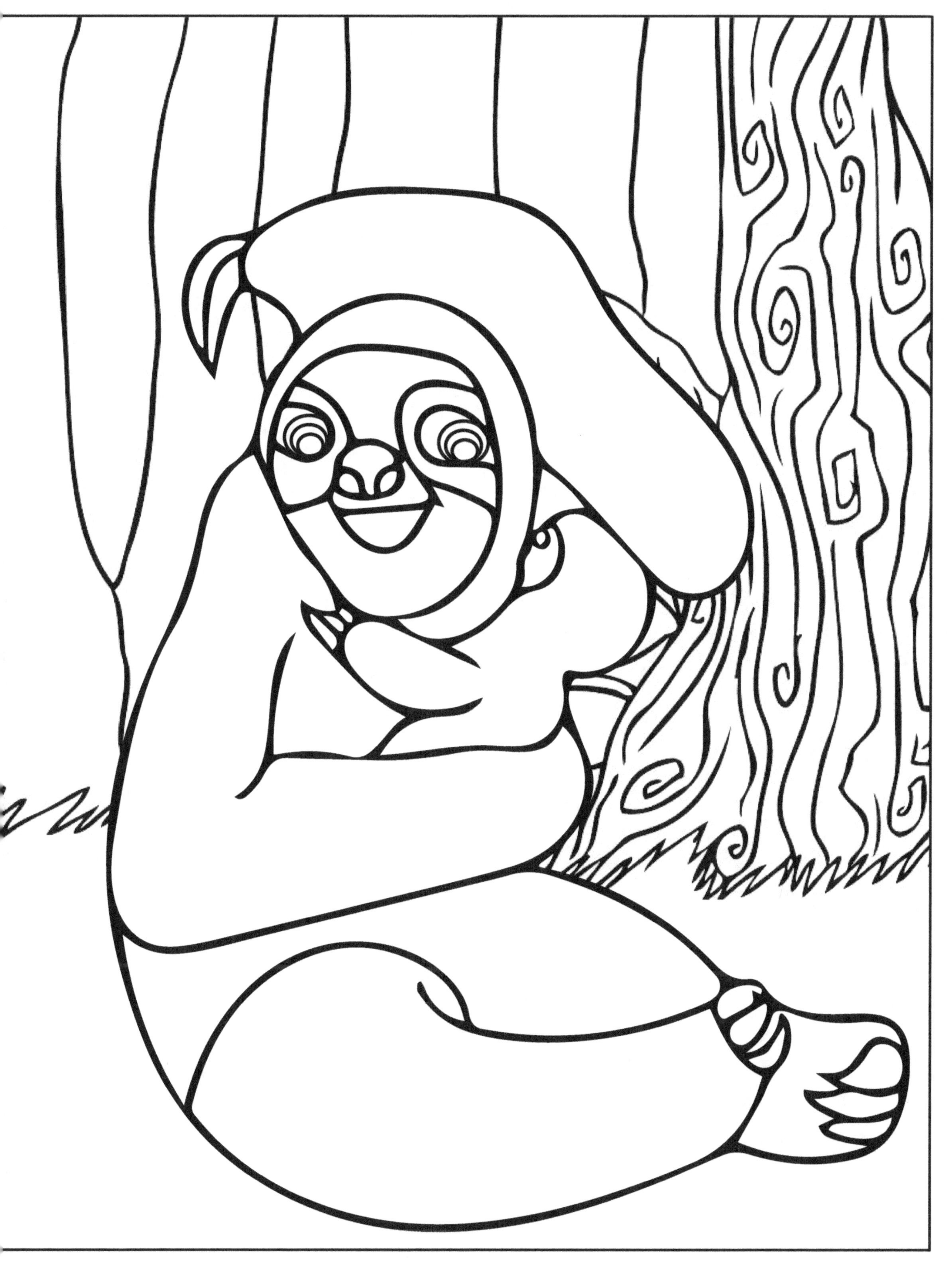

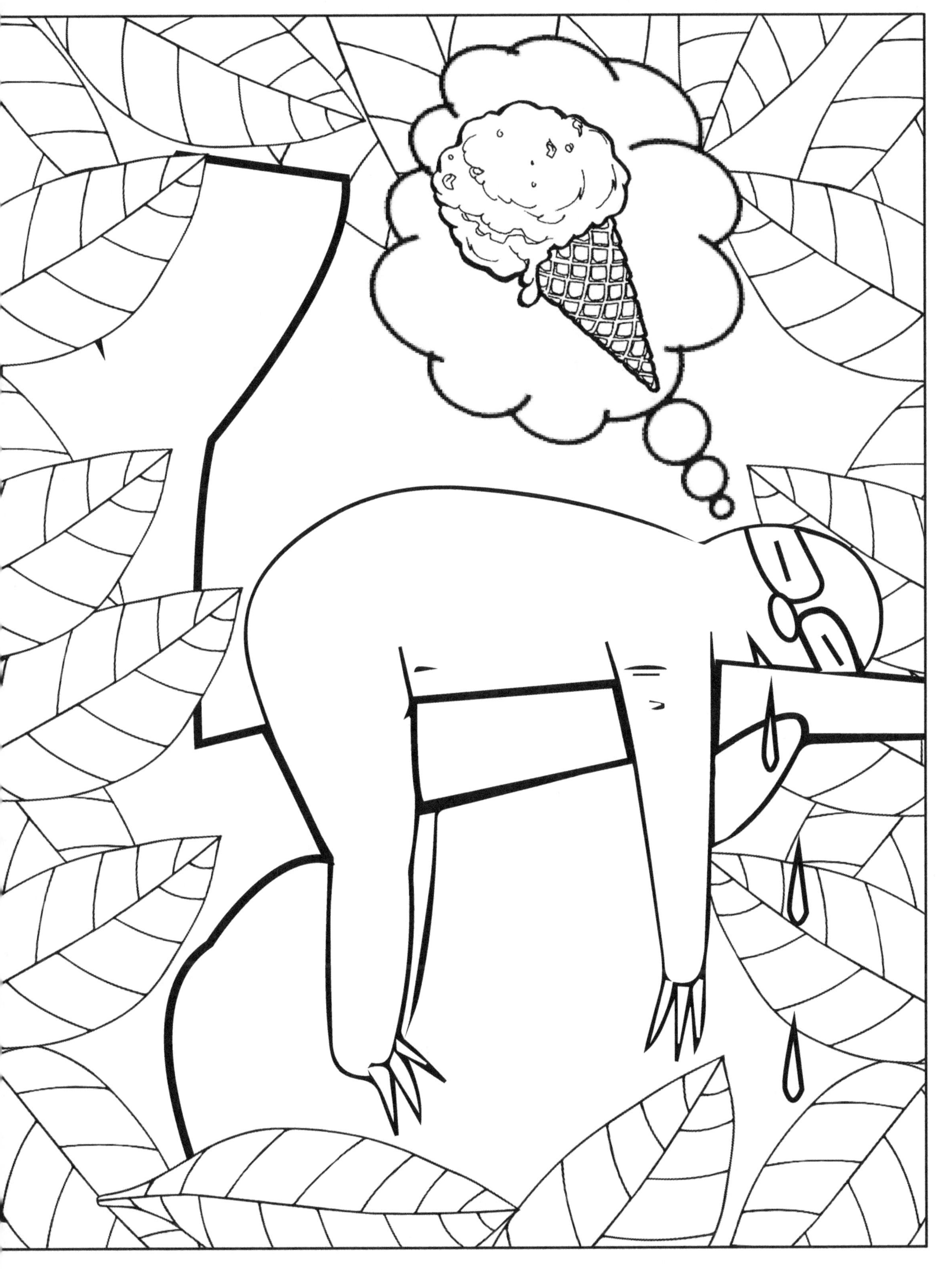

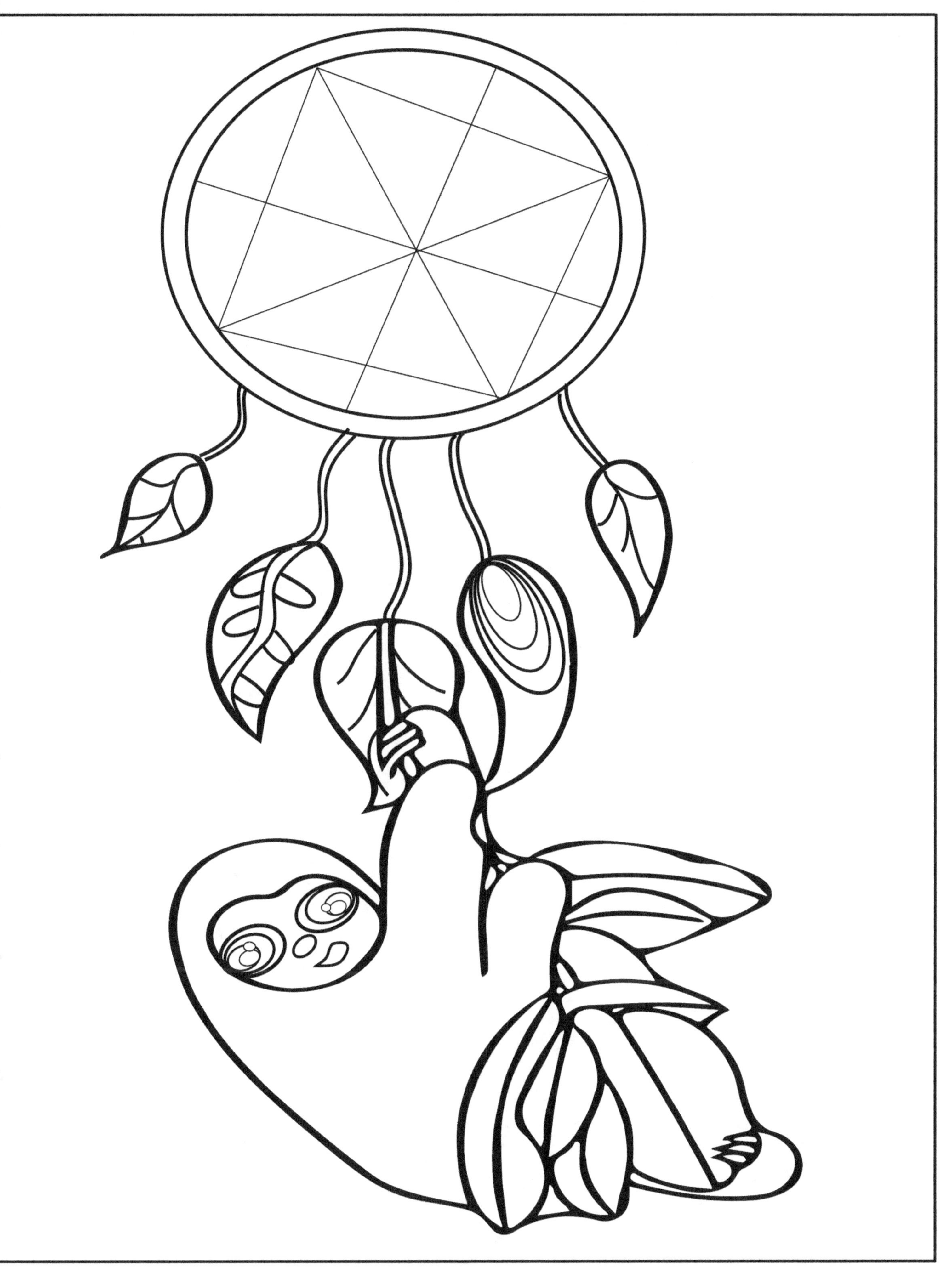

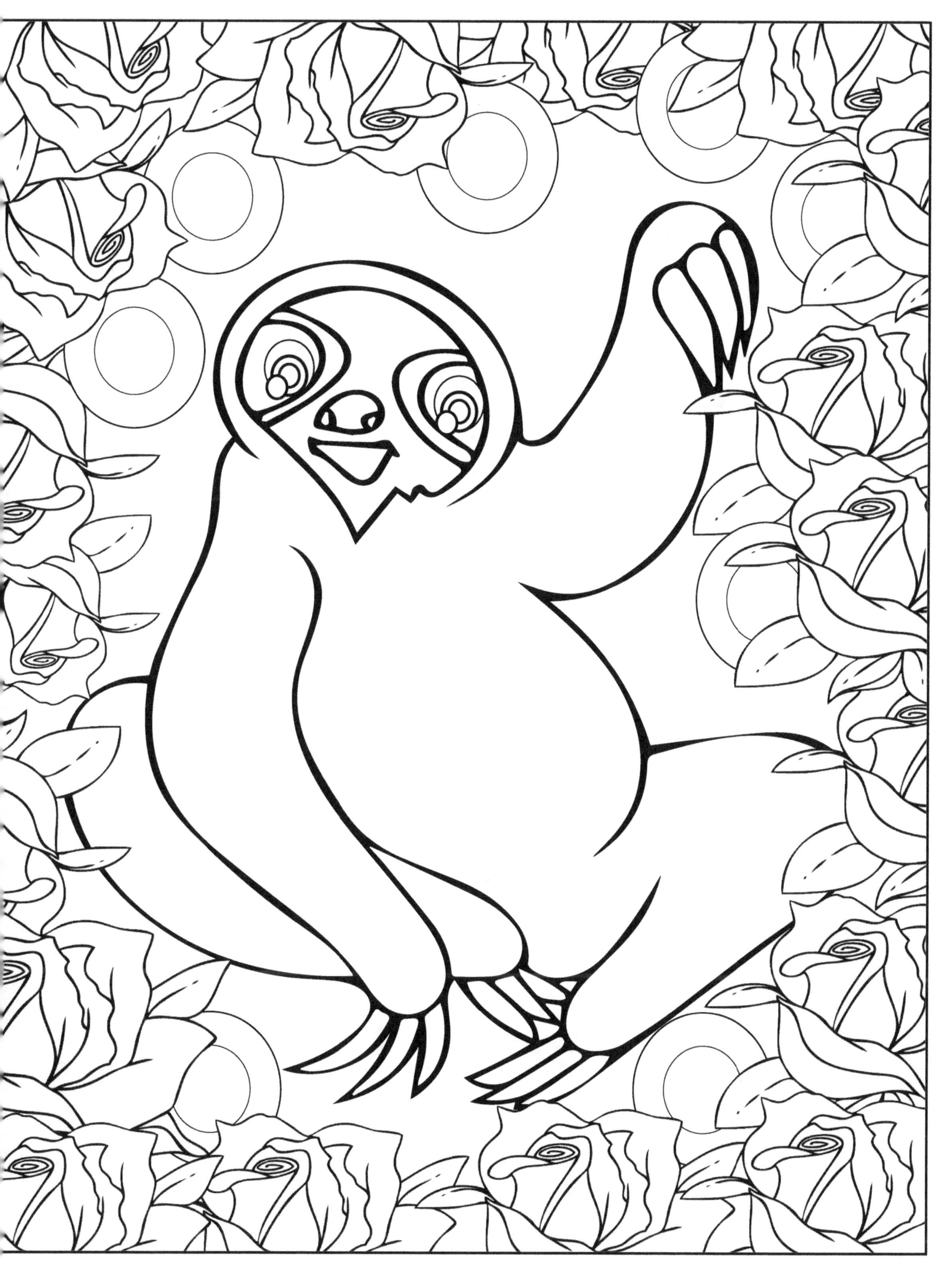

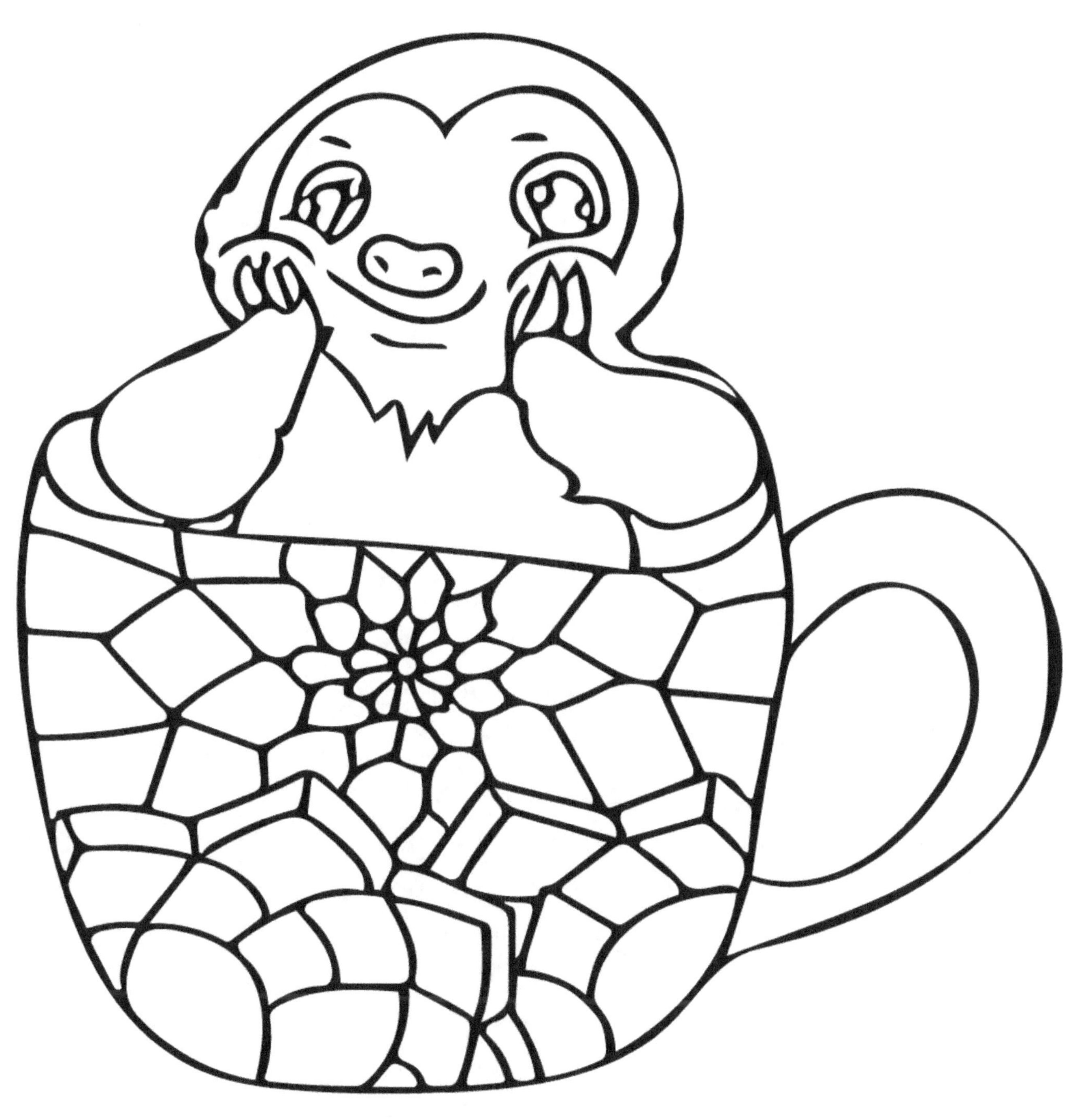

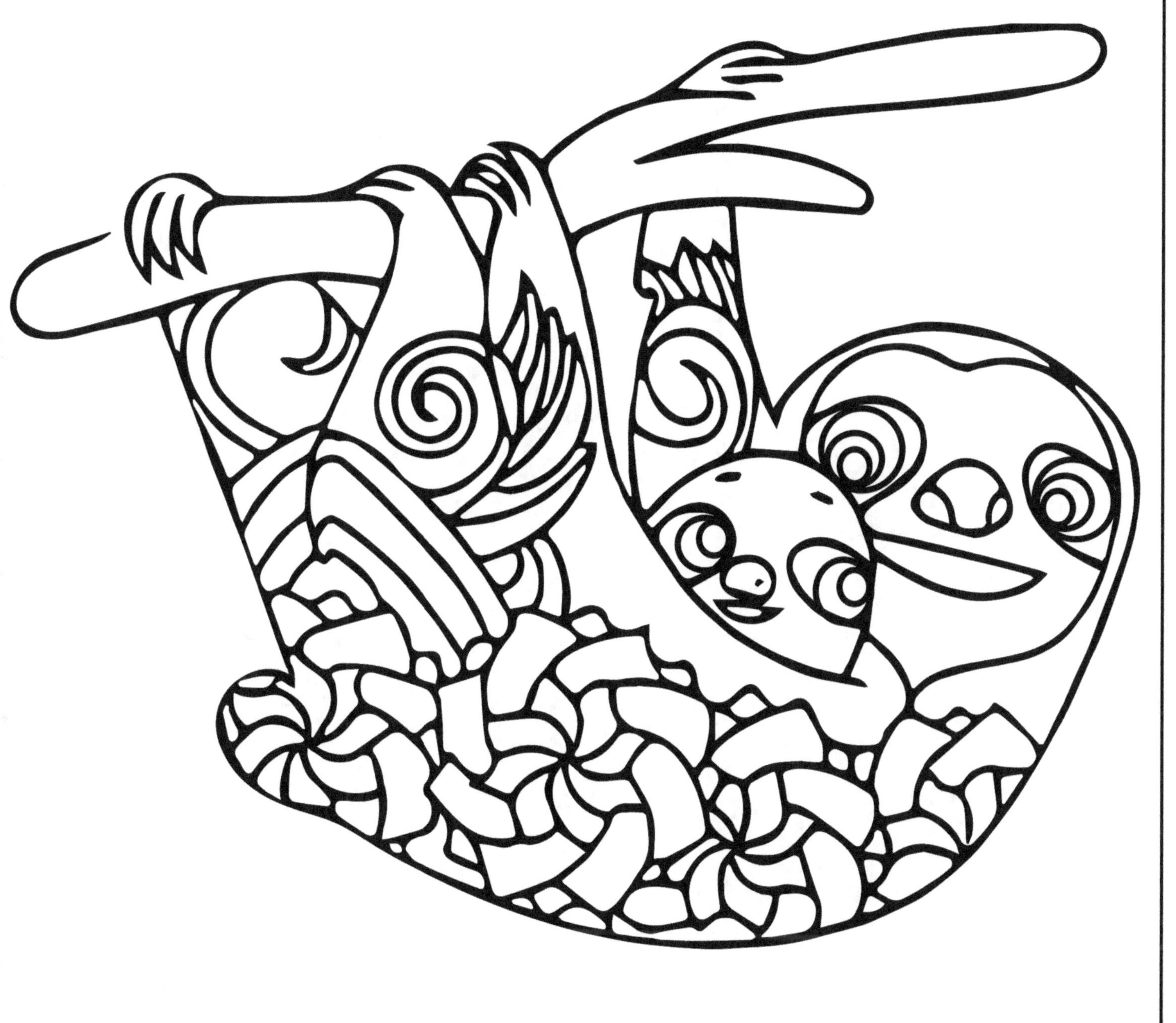

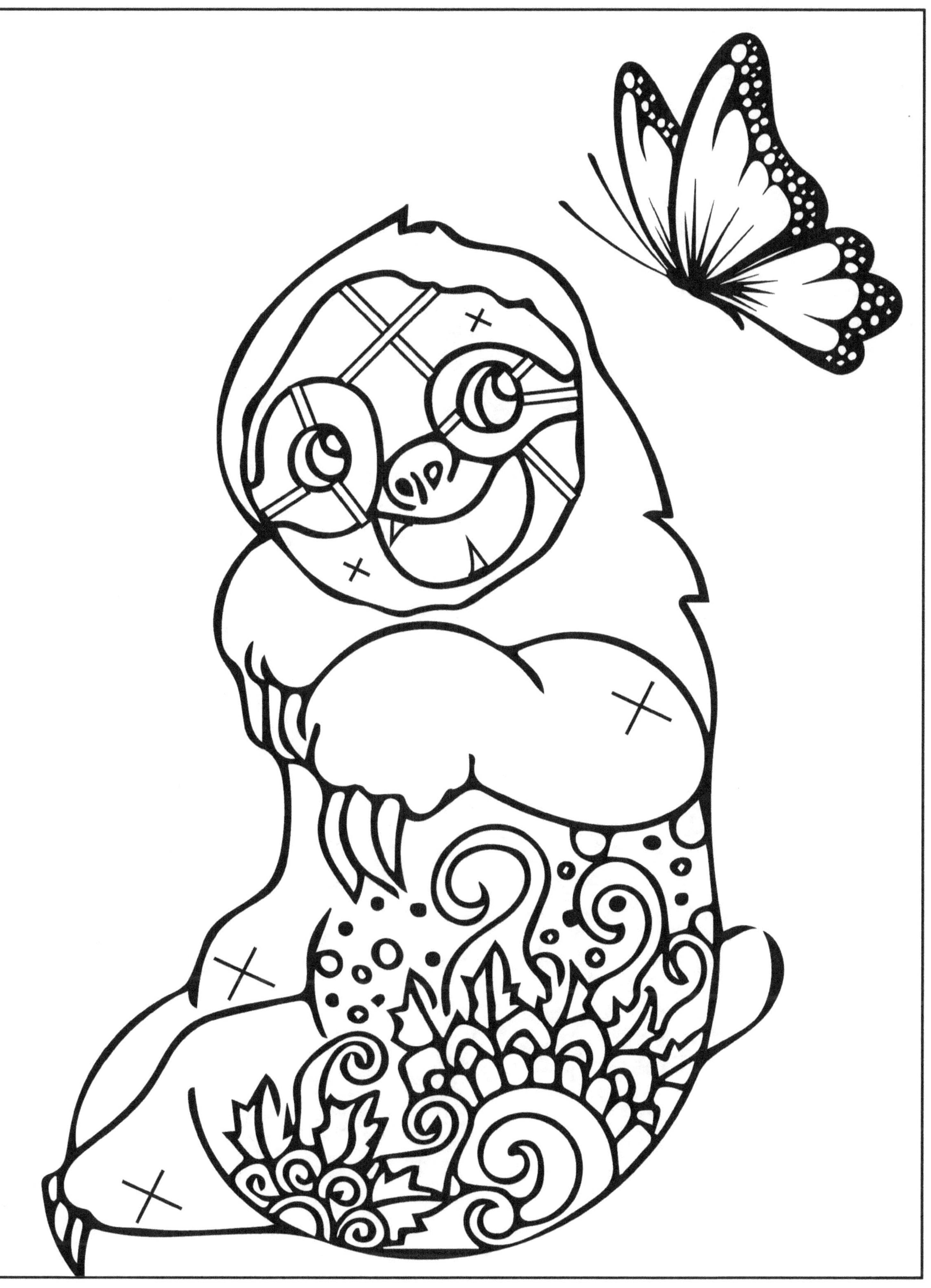

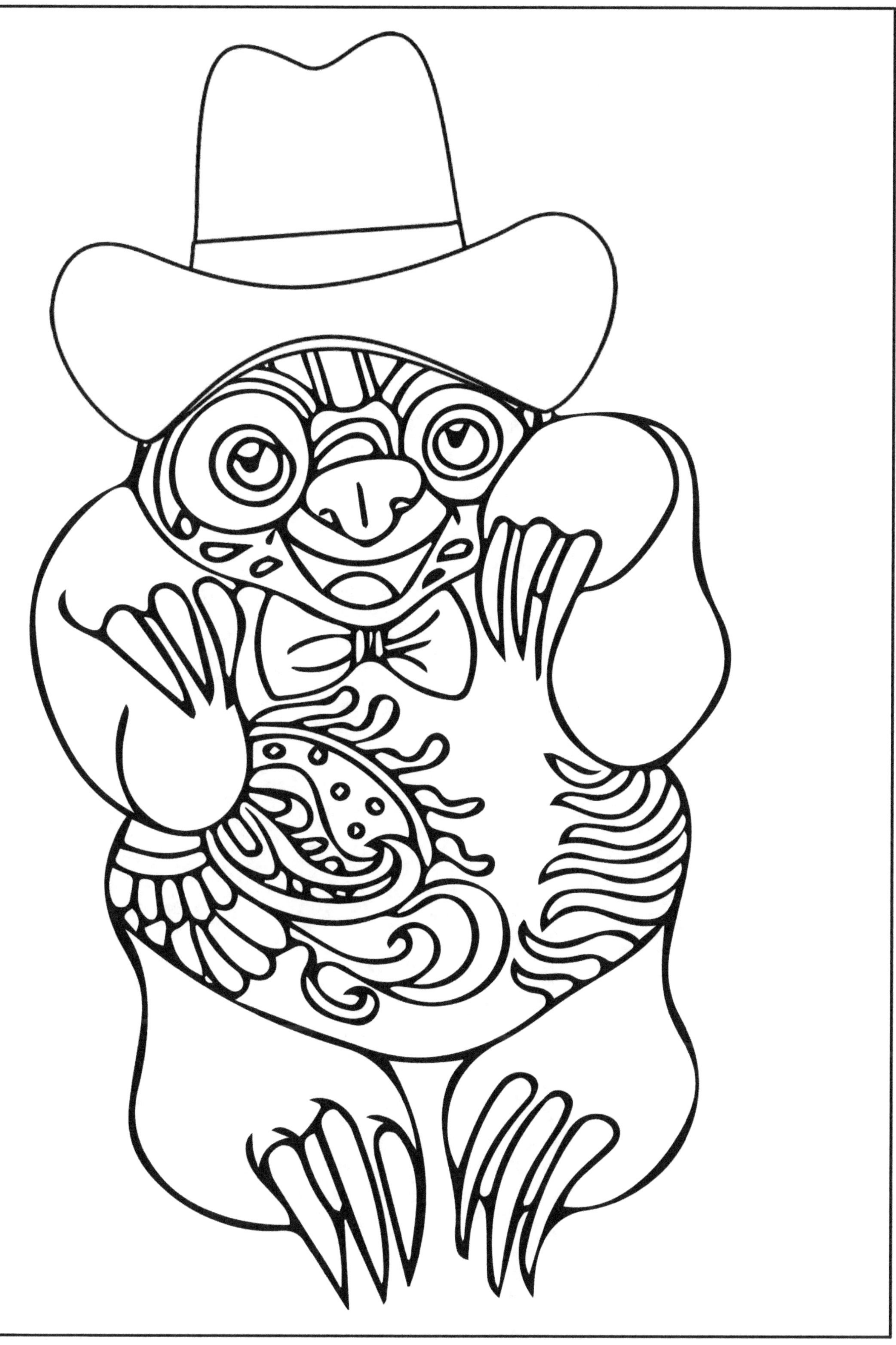

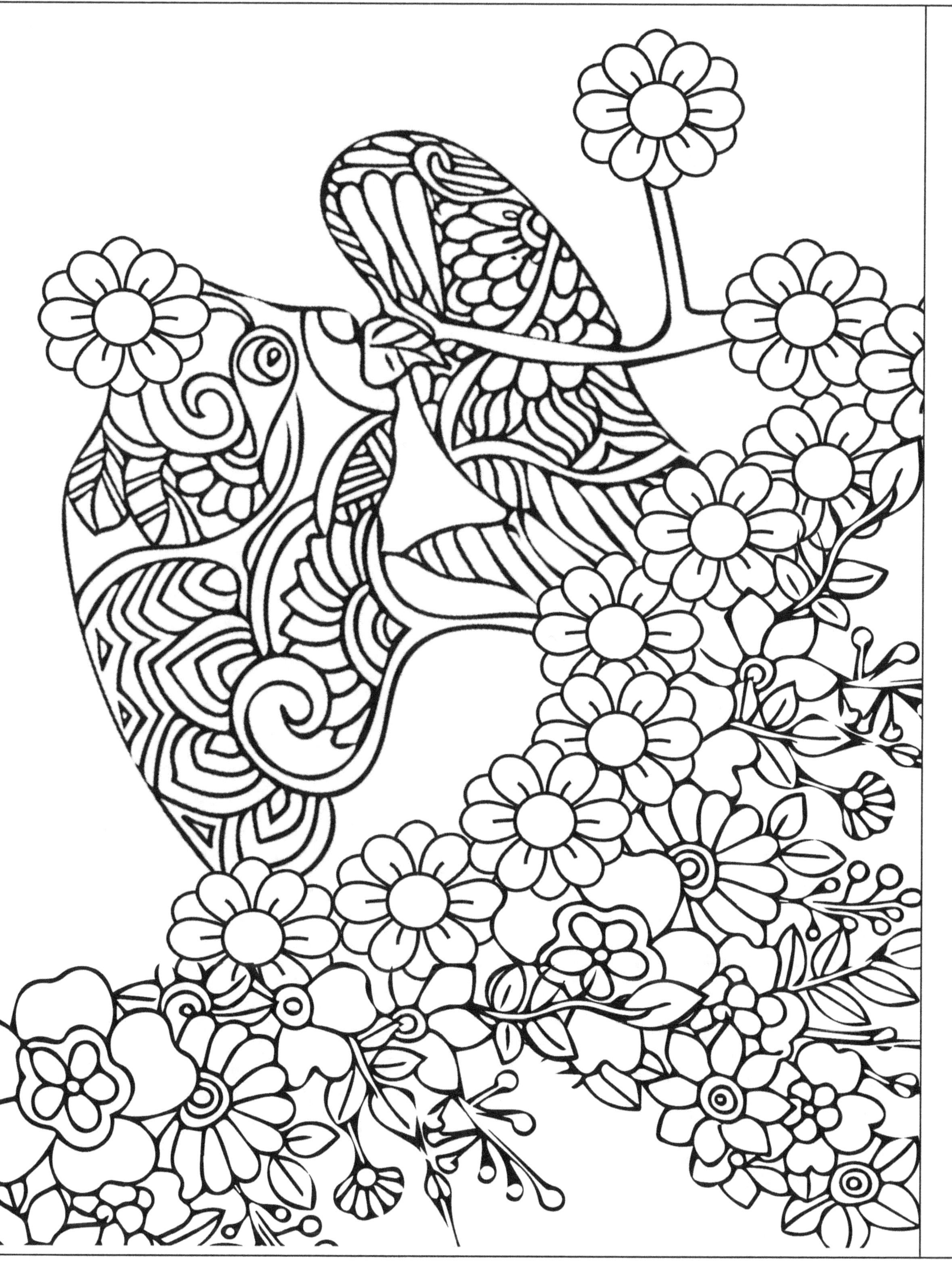

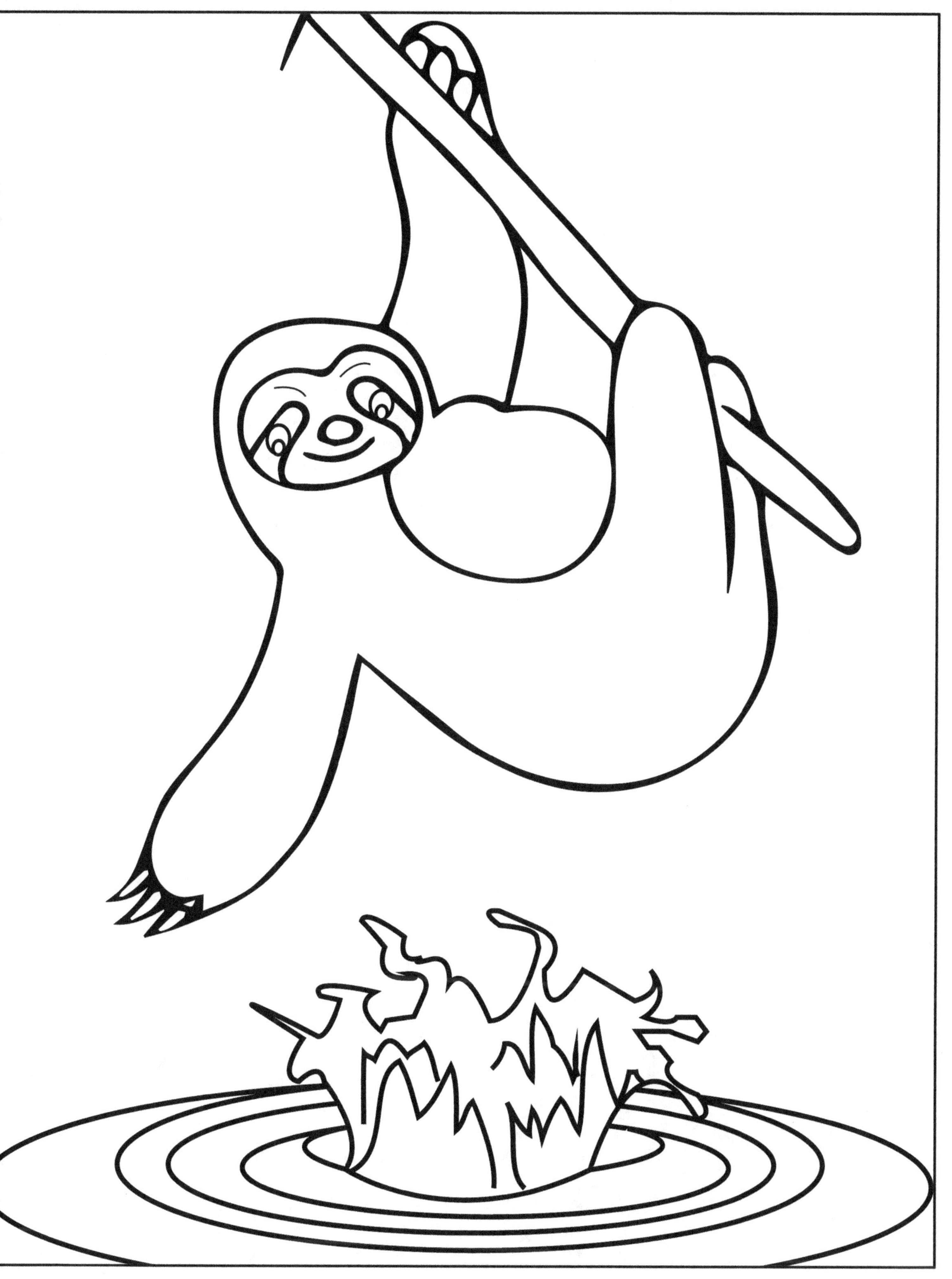

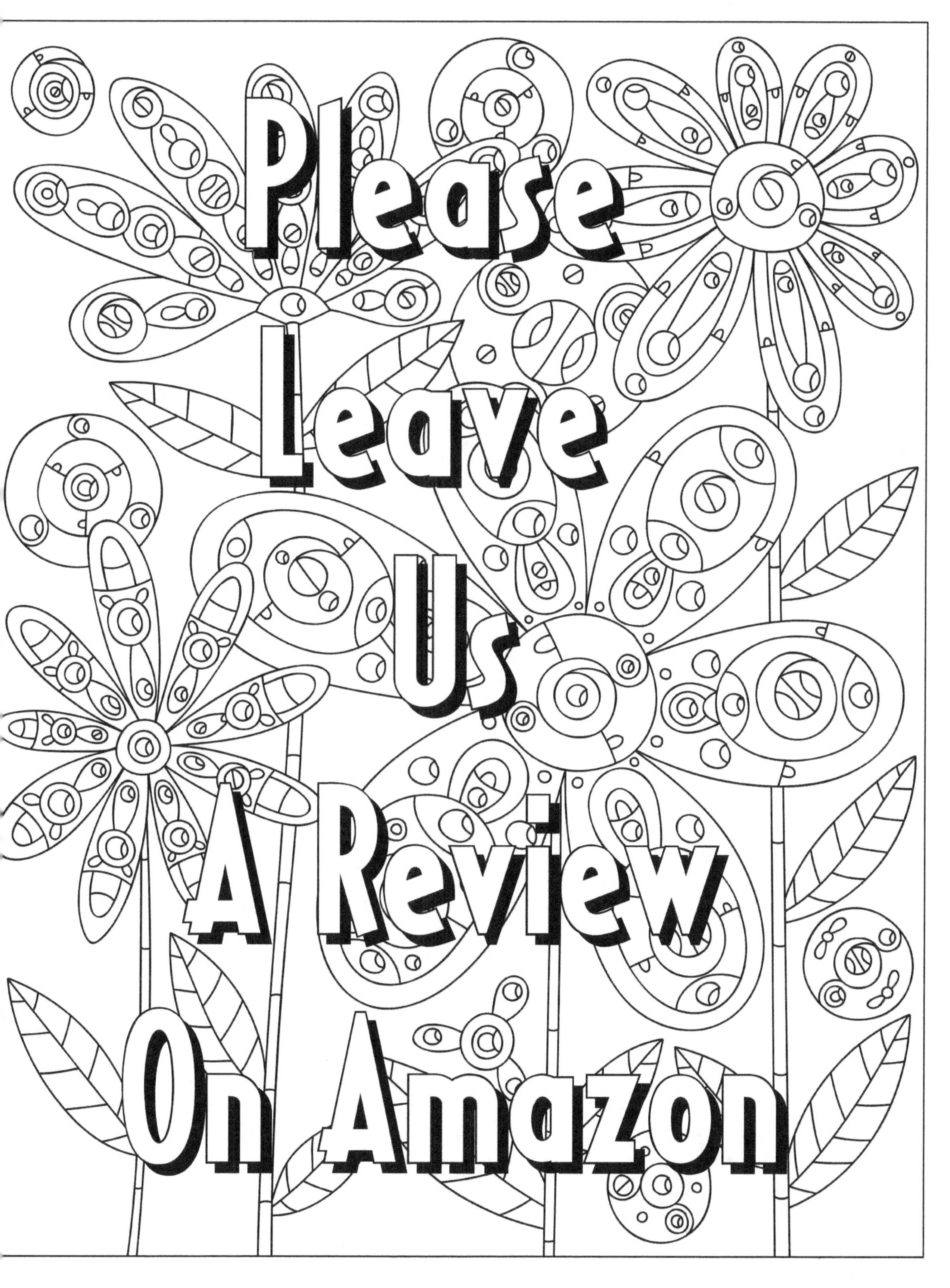

Please
Leave
Us
A Review
On Amazon